A Grammar Companion
for Primary Teachers

A Grammar Companion

FOR PRIMARY TEACHERS

BEVERLY DEREWIANKA

Primary English Teaching Association

First published November 1998
Reprinted December 1999, February 2001, January 2002, December 2002, May 2004
Copyright © Primary English Teaching Association
and Beverly Derewianka
Laura Street, Newtown NSW 2042 Australia

Copying for Educational Purposes

Copying for other purposes

National Library of Australia Cataloguing-in-Publication data

Beverly Derewianka, 1946-

A grammar companion for primary teachers
ISBN 1 87 5622 30 6

1. English language – Grammar – Study and teaching (Primary).
2. Grammar, Comparative and general – study and teaching (Primary).
I. Primary English Teaching Association (Australia). II. Title.

415

Edited by Rosamund Else-Mitchell
Cover and text design by Rebecca Webster, Oracle Desktop Designs
Illustrations by Anna Webster, Oracle Desktop Designs
Typeset in Goudy by Oracle Desktop Designs
Printed at Ligare Pty Ltd
138 Bonds Road Riverwood NSW 2210

THIS BOOK IS DEDICATED TO THE
MEMORY OF VLADIMIR DEREWIANKA—
WHO WAS CONSTANTLY INTRIGUED BY
THE POSSIBILITIES OF LANGUAGE.

Preface

Over the past few years, PETA has published a number of books dealing directly or indirectly with questions of grammar. In the widely-read *Exploring How Texts Work* (1990) by Beverly Derewianka certain grammatical features were highlighted in terms of how they operated within particular genres. This provided insights into how grammar could be treated functionally in context. John Collerson followed this up with a more detailed account of English grammar from a functional perspective in *English Grammar: A Functional Approach* (1994). This work was groundbreaking, introducing teachers to a different way of looking at language based on Halliday's functional grammar. In 1997, PETA published John Collerson's *Grammar in Teaching* which demonstrated a rich variety of ways in which functional grammar could be drawn upon in classroom activities.

So why do we need another book on grammar? The increasing interest in grammar throughout Australia and its appearance in a number of syllabus and curriculum documents has stimulated a demand for a handbook which familiarises teachers with the basics of the English grammatical system. While teachers have been excited by the potential of working with a functional approach to grammar, many are still a bit daunted by its newness and the terminology. This book is intended therefore as a bridge for teachers between what they already know about grammar and how they might extend that knowledge to include a more functional perspective.

A Grammar Companion for Primary Teachers is a reference book, systematically outlining the different grammatical features of English at the level of the word, the group, the clause, the sentence and the text. It employs terminology which is familiar to teachers and the community, but where necessary it uses terms which allow for a more functional interpretation. It endorses the underlying principles and the approach to grammar outlined by Collerson and—with a slight shift in terminology—can be used in conjunction with his suggestions for classroom practice in *Grammar in Teaching*.

We are sure that *A Grammar Companion* will become a well-thumbed reference and guide which will truly keep you company and provide reassurance as you introduce children to the fascinating workings of grammar.

Publications Editor
Primary English Teaching Association

Acknowledgements

The author would like to express her appreciation of the many stimulating discussions about language in general and grammar in particular involving teachers, students, and academic colleagues. In particular, she would like to thank Michael Halliday for his inspiration and Geoff Williams, Jim Martin, David Butt and Clare Painter for their helpful suggestions. Thanks also need to go to the tireless PETA staff, to Rosamund Else-Mitchell for her fine editing and Rebecca Webster for her clean design and hard work.

Acknowledgement is due to copyright holders: authors and publishers for their kind permission to include extracts, as referenced on page 123. While every effort has been made to trace copyright holders in some cases this has proved impossible. In the event of a copyright query, please contact the publishers.

Contents

Introduction

What is grammar?

Grammar is a way of describing how a language works to make meaning within a particular culture.

Why learn about grammar?

- to be able to reflect on how the English language works
- to have a shared language for talking about the main features of the English language
- to understand how grammatical structures create different kinds of meaning
- to examine patterns of language and word choices to critically analyse texts
- to be able to use language effectively, appropriately and accurately.

Assumptions

The approach to grammar adopted in this book is based on the following assumptions:

- Language is a dynamic, complex system of resources for making meaning. Students should be encouraged to explore it as a fascinating phenomenon which is central to their lives.
- Language reflects the culture in which it is used. It is not a neutral medium, but expresses certain world-views, values, beliefs and attitudes.
- Language changes from situation to situation, depending on the social purpose for which it is being used, the subject matter, who is involved, and whether the language is spoken or written.
- The emphasis in language study is on how people use authentic language in various contexts in real life to achieve their purposes. The particular focus will be on the language needed for successful participation in school contexts.
- A knowledge of grammar can help us to critically evaluate our own texts and those of others (eg identifying point of view; examining how language can be manipulated to achieve certain effects and position the reader in a particular way; knowing how language can be used to construct a particular identity or a particular way of viewing the world).

- The approach to grammar should not have the effect of excluding or marginalising students who speak a social dialect which is different from Standard Australian English. Different varieties of English are to be respected and maintained, while extending the students' ability to use appropriate registers in specific situations (eg written texts in school and workplace contexts).

A multi-purpose grammar

The description of grammar provided here has been designed so that teachers can use it for a number of different purposes: for understanding the structure or formation of various language features; for anticipating where students might need particular assistance with certain features; and for exploring how language functions to create different types of meaning. Throughout the book, these different purposes have been signalled by the use of visual cues—the symbols and screen discussed on the following pages.

◉ Looking at meaning

While knowledge about the structure of language can be informative and useful, these days it is not generally seen as an end in itself. In this book, we look at how the different grammatical categories are involved in the construction of meaning:

- what jobs do adverbials do? what happens if I leave them out?
- how can my choice of nouns affect the meaning of the text?
- how can I use certain types of adjectives to express my opinion about something?
- which grammatical categories are involved in skills such as classifying, defining, describing, categorising, exemplifying?
- which linguistic features can help me form a text which is coherent and cohesive?
- how do the grammatical patterns change from text to text? why? with what effect?
- how do the grammatical choices in literary texts differ from factual texts?
- how does the context affect the sort of grammatical choices made?

Here we are viewing grammar as a resource—an array of possibilities from which we can choose. Learning grammar in this sense is seen as extending a learner's potential to make and produce meanings. A functional approach to language is concerned with the language choices available to construct different kinds of meanings and how these choices vary according to the social context.

⊞ *Formation*

A traditional motive for teaching about grammar has been the development of an analytical approach to language—an ability to 'reason grammatically', and a metalinguistic awareness. Being able to identify and name different grammatical categories provides students with a language for talking about language. Knowing how language is structured helps us to deal with questions such as:

- how are prefixes and suffixes used to create words?
- what does a noun group contain?
- how are different verb tenses formed?
- what does a clause look like?
- how are messages combined to form sentences?

Once students are conscious of how different linguistic structures are formed, they are in a better position to be able to manipulate these structures to create clear, well-structured, unambiguous sentences. And in their reading, they are better able to perceive meaningful 'chunks' of language rather than to read each word as a discrete unit.

Troubleshooting

There are certain linguistic structures which often cause problems for young students. In many cases, the problems will sort themselves out over time. Often, however, it is useful for the teacher to be able to identify trouble spots so that the problem can be explained or so that activities can be designed to address the difficulty.

It is this area which many people associate with the learning of grammar: the correction of 'mistakes'. This is a legitimate area of concern. Students' language is often judged by their control over certain linguistic features, and this can be a significant factor in examinations, job applications, and so on. It is important, however, not to let this get out of perspective. There are probably only a dozen or so "problem structures" which regularly crop up in children's writing.

Bridging approaches

In a truly functional grammar, you would need to have two layers of terminology: one to describe the grammatical category and one to describe the different functions which the grammatical category can perform. This is important, as each grammatical category can do a variety of jobs. There is no one-to-one correspondence between form and function. A noun, for example, can represent a participant in an action, or it can express a particular viewpoint, or it can act as the theme of a sentence, or it can help to make links within a text.

In Collerson's grammar (1994), the starting point was function and meaning, with less emphasis on the grammatical categories used to realise the meanings. In this book the starting point is the grammatical categories, working towards the different kinds of meanings which they can make.

Ideally, students should be familiar both with terms which refer to form (eg noun, verb) and terms which refer to their functions (eg participant, process). At this stage, however, it is seen as a useful interim strategy to draw on teachers' current knowledge about grammar and extend that to include a functional perspective. This has been done here by using conventional terminology where possible (eg 'verb'), by incorporating functional aspects through the use of terms such as 'action verb', 'saying verb', 'thinking verb', and by using functional terms where there is no equivalent in more traditional grammars (eg 'theme', 'cohesive link').

A functional perspective

A functional approach looks at how language enables us to do things in our daily lives. To participate successfully in school and the community, for example, students need to know how to use language:

- for achieving different social purposes
- for interacting with others
- for developing understandings about the world
- and for moving from 'more spoken' to 'more written' forms

Achieving different social purposes

As they progress through school and life, learners need to be able to use language in order to achieve a range of social purposes: describing, explaining, arguing, recounting, and so on. These different social purposes are expressed through different text-types. Young children operate with a moderate range of text types which generally have a relatively basic, unelaborated structure (eg recounts involving only a couple of events, arguments that are unsupported by evidence, explanations of only a sentence or two in length). With teacher guidance over the years, students should be able to confidently interpret and employ a wide range of text types for a variety of social purposes, including texts which have a more complex, unpredictable structure. This provides students with a solid preparation for the demands of secondary school and life in the community.

While not dealing in detail with different genres or text types, this book will refer to how different grammatical resources are drawn on in achieving different social purposes.

Interacting with others

One of the major functions of language is to enable interaction. Through language we construct particular roles and relationships. Students need to be able to use language effectively to interact with a range of people. In the early years, they will use language in more informal, familiar ways with known peers and adults, freely expressing their feelings and attitudes. Gradually they will also need to learn ways of expressing themselves that are a bit more formal and detached, with a more subtle use of evaluative language and modality, particularly in the written mode.

In school, children need the skills of group interaction, the ability to take part in class discussions, the poise to talk with both familiar and unfamiliar adults. They need to know how to cope in situations with different degrees of authority and power (eg in terms of expertise, age, gender, ethnicity). They need to know how to take on an expanding range of roles: group leader, observer, apprentice, mediator, initiator, questioner, co-learner. They need to be able to evaluate their own interaction skills and to reflect critically on the ways in which others use language to interact with them in oral and written language (eg are they being persuaded to accept a particular point of view? how is language being used to do this? how might they recognise this and resist if necessary?). In many cases, children will need explicit assistance in developing these interpersonal skills.

This book will provide examples of how different grammatical categories are involved when making statements, asking questions, giving commands, expressing opinions, making judgements, and so on. This is called the interpersonal function of language.

Representing experience

Another major function of language is to represent the world, to help us to express and understand our experiences. In the school context, this involves using and understanding the language of the different areas of the curriculum. It is now well-known that each subject has its own way of using language to develop knowledge and understandings relevant to that area. The language of science, for example, is quite different from the language of history. The language used in English literary texts is quite different from that of mathematics texts. Students need to be able to read and write texts which become increasingly technical and subject-specific as they move through the school system from primary to high school.

On entering school, students' language will be concerned with more particular, everyday understandings ('my family', 'our neighbourhood'). As they grow older, they need to be able to talk and write in more generalised terms ('families', 'dinosaurs') about less familiar topics which often require research ('the planets', 'volcano eruptions') and specialist terminology ('solar system', 'lava'). It cannot be taken for granted that this type of language will develop automatically.

This book will include examples of how grammar functions to represent our experience of the world: the kinds of activities taking place, the participants in those activities, the circumstances surrounding those activities, and the relationship between ideas.

Creating oral and written texts

One of the major shifts in children's language use over the primary years is from the spoken mode to the written mode. When students enter school, they are accustomed to using language in face-to-face oral interaction. It is spontaneous and immediate. It generally refers to the 'here-and-now', to the surrounding context. There is an interaction partner who can provide support by asking questions, giving feedback, requesting clarification. When moving to the written mode, students need to learn how to use language in quite different ways. Texts will involve a degree of planning, revising and reworking and will therefore be more highly structured. Because the writer has more time to construct the text, the sentences are generally more 'crafted', with greater complexity and density.

Because a written text needs to be able to 'stand on its own', the reader cannot get help from an interaction partner or the surrounding setting. The reader must use cues from the text itself to undertand how it is developing. And the writer needs to know how to guide the reader through the text. This involves quite sophisticated language skills (eg using the beginning focus of the sentence or clause, using text connectives, compacting information so that it does not sound 'rambling'). Moving successfully from spoken to written modes is one of the major achievements of primary schooling, requiring the development of a number of high-level skills and strategies. Children who cannot cope with the features of written text have great difficulties in later schooling.

This book deals with the language features involved in constructing coherent and cohesive texts.

The following diagram summarises how the different language functions are involved in students' learning through the primary school.

EARLY CHILDHOOD   **LATER CHILDHOOD**

Language for achieving different purposes

producing and interpreting small range of text-types with basic structures for specific purposes	producing and interpreting greater range of text-types, with more complex structures (multiple purposes, less predictable stages)

Language for interacting with others

◄───►

| operating in contexts which involve more personal, informal, familiar interaction; free expression of judgement and assertiveness; and a limited range of roles | operating in contexts which include more impersonal, formal, careful expression of judgement and assertiveness; expanded range of roles; critical awareness of how language can be used to position self and others. |

Language for representing experience

◄───►

| dealing with everyday, individualised, concrete, non-specialised subject matter | dealing with more technical, generalised, abstract, discipline-specific subject matter |

Language for creating oral and written texts

◄───►

| engaging in face-to-face, spontaneous, context-dependent dialogues | distanced—in time and space— monologic, crafted and planned, independent of immediate context |

Considerations for teaching grammar

Most children will learn how to use grammar implicitly by engaging in extensive and purposeful talking, listening, reading, writing and viewing. Children come to school with a highly-developed ability to use language in rich and complex ways. Their language will continue to develop naturally as they use it for a variety of purposes in their homes, in the community and school. In addition to this natural acquisition, this book will assume that the teacher plays a deliberate role in enhancing children's language use in certain areas and in developing their awareness of language.

Learning to ...

In the classroom, children will be learning to use language in particular ways. The teacher's role is to design contexts and plan activities in all curriculum areas which provide opportunities for children to develop the particular language they need in order to participate effectively in school. The teacher's knowledge about language will assist in selecting resources, choosing texts, focusing on salient points, constructing language-rich activities, responding to questions, assessing students' work, and providing informed feedback. At the end of each section of the book, you will find a description of how children—with teacher guidance—might be using the particular language feature at various stages. This is not intended as a benchmark, but rather as an indication of directions in which teachers might actively promote children's language use.

Learning about ...

In addition to fostering children's ability to *use* language in particular ways, the teacher can tap into the child's implicit knowledge about language and help make it more explicit. The teacher can provide learners with tools for reflecting on how language works. Together they build up a shared language for talking about language (a 'metalanguage') so that they can refer to the various features and structures of language. During activities such as shared and guided reading, modelled and collaborative writing, conferencing, as part of the editing process, in class discussions, and so on, the teacher is able to focus on how language is functioning. By selecting certain texts, modelling relevant features, highlighting specific points, asking particular questions, the teacher draws their attention to ways in which language is being used. In this way the teacher is able to demonstrate how grammar is contributing to the meaning of the text. At the end of each section, you will find suggestions as to the kind of knowledge about language which children might be guided throughout their primary schooling.

Grammar should generally be taught in the context of working with whole texts (eg identifying grammatical patterns which help a particular text-type achieve its purpose). The emphasis should not be on the ability simply to label a particular feature, but on its usefulness in creating, appreciating and evaluating texts. Students should be shown how grammar helps to build up the meaning of the text. When dealing with information reports, for example, you might want to demonstrate how the timeless present tense is used for generalising. This can then be contrasted with the specific actions in the past found in recounts. The texts used when teaching grammar should be authentic, not artificial and contrived simply to teach a grammatical point. They may, however, need to be simplified, when first introducing a certain feature.

There are times, however, when it might be more efficient to look at a particular, relevant aspect of grammar more intensively. For example, if a specific feature is presenting particular challenges, then additional language activities on that feature could be explored, using a number of clear examples taken from texts.

Certain groups of students will need more systematic and focused assistance with particular features of English grammar, eg students from non-English-speaking backgrounds. Emphasis should be placed on the construction of clear, well-formed, and coherent sentences and texts, and not so much on the rules of usage (eg split infinitives, the use of 'shall').

Teachers need to use their own judgement as to how much information or detail the students can usefully and comfortably deal with at any particular time. The grammatical features outlined in this book should serve as a guide as to what might reasonably be learned by most children during the years of primary schooling.

The study of grammar need not be onerous or dry. There is room for playfulness and creativity, for experimentation and discovery, for enjoyment and wonder. Children have an instinctive fascination with language. It is the teacher's job to nurture this.

Levels of grammar

When we are teaching grammar, we need to be clear about which level we are dealing with. The diagram on page 10 illustrates the levels described below and the relationships between them.

Text

Modern grammars now recognise how grammar extends beyond the sentence and can operate at the level of the whole text. At the text level, we find grammatical patterns which are related to a particular text type (eg the use of commands in a procedure, the use of action verbs in a recount, the use of abstract nouns in an exposition, the use of dialogue in a narrative). We also find certain features which serve to link a text together: cohesive devices such as pronouns, words which show relationships within the text (eg synonyms, repeated words), words which signal how the text is structured (eg Firstly ... ; On the one hand ...).

Sentence

A text is made up of a number of sentences. Sentences can consist of a single clause or a number of clauses joined together. A sentence may be a statement, a question, or a command. Students need to know how to combine clauses and how to show the relationship between clauses in a sentence.

Clause

A clause is a unit of meaning which expresses a message. It must contain a verb. The clause is often seen as the basic unit for analysing language.

Group/Phrase

A clause consists of smaller 'chunks' or groups of words which do certain jobs. At the core of the clause is the verb group (eg **'was playing'**). Involved in this action might be one or more persons or things, represented by a noun group (eg '**The frisky white kitten** was playing'). There might also be some extra information in the form of an adverbial (eg 'The frisky white kitten was playing **in the hallway**').

Word

Groups and phrases can be divided into individual words. In a noun group, for example, we might find an article, an adjective and a noun (eg the wily fox). It is important to see how individual words function within a group so that students can see how the words relate to each other.

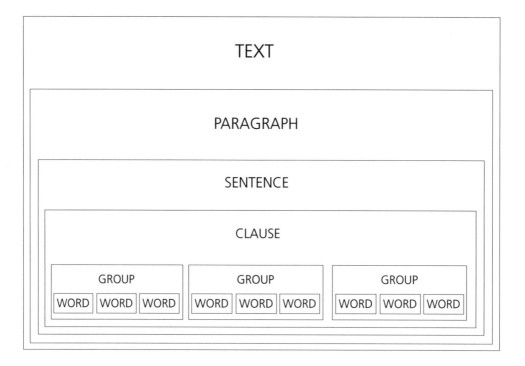

In the past, grammar was often taught at the level of the individual word, eg 'noun', 'verb', 'preposition'. While these categories are important, students often ended up with a fragmented knowledge of the system, with little idea of how these words work together to make meaning.

In the following four sections we will look at the larger 'chunks': those words and groups of words which make up a clause.

The clause

The basic unit of meaning in English is the clause. A clause conveys a message. In terms of representing the world, a clause provides information about

- what is happening
- who is taking part
- the circumstances surrounding the activity (when? where? how? etc)

What is happening?

We could say that a clause represents a slice of experience. Our experiences are generally made up of 'doings' and 'happenings', so at the heart of the clause is a **verb**. (Sometimes this is called a **verb group** because it can contain more than one word.)

If we look at this picture, we can see several things happening:

VERB
(or **verb group**)

The girl bear	**is rolling**	the dough.
The baby bear	**is about to lick**	the spoon.
The boy bear	**has been making**	a gingerbread man.
The kettle	**is boiling**.	

A common way of identifying a clause is to look for the verb group representing the process. Generally each clause must have a verb in order to be classed as a clause.

Who (or what) is taking part?

Actions don't just happen. They involve people, places, things, ideas and so on. In the picture above, we can see a number of participants in the actions. These are represented by nouns.

NOUN (or **noun group**)		NOUN (or **noun group**)
The girl bear	is rolling	**the dough.**
The baby bear	is about to lick	**the spoon.**
The boy bear	has been making	**a gingerbread man.**
The kettle	is boiling.	

Sometimes these are called **noun groups** because they can contain more than one word. The noun 'kettle' for example can be expanded into a noun group by adding various describers:

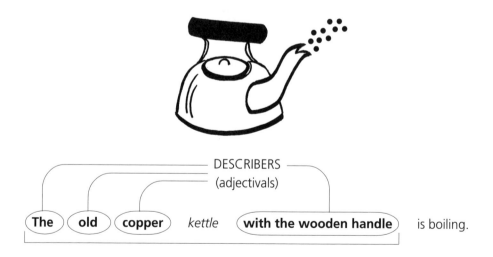

More technically, we could use the word **adjectivals** for these various types of noun describers. Noun groups are discussed in the following section.

What are the surrounding circumstances?

Sometimes we want more information about an action. We want to know about such circumstances as:

- where?
- when?
- how?
- why?

These details are usually expressed through various types of verb describers. We can group these together using the term **adverbial**, that is, any word or group of words which tells us more about the verb.

Look back at the picture of the bears in the kitchen. We can provide extra information about the actions by using adverbials:

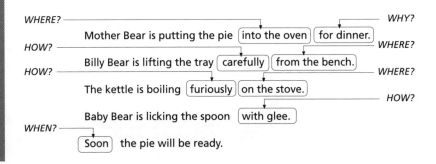

Summary

To put it very simply, we could say that most grammatical features in the clause cluster around (i) the noun and (ii) the verb. Those words which provide more information about nouns we could call 'noun describers' (or more technically, adjectivals) and those words which provide more information about verbs we could call 'verb describers' (or more technically, adverbials):

In terms of meaning,

- **nouns** answer questions such as 'who?' or 'what?'

- **adjectivals** answer questions such as 'which one?', 'whose?', 'what's it like?', 'how many?', 'what type?'

- **verbs** answer questions such as 'what's happening?'

- **adverbials** answer questions such as 'when?', 'where?', 'how?', 'why?'

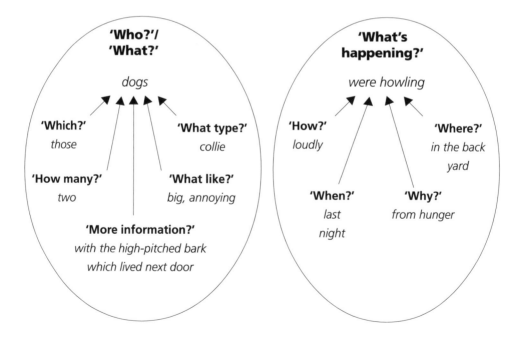

These four major categories (nouns, adjectivals, verbs and adverbials) are used in clauses in a variety of combinations. Generally, adjectivals combine with nouns to form noun groups, but adverbials tend to move more freely around the clause and are not seen as part of the verb group, eg:

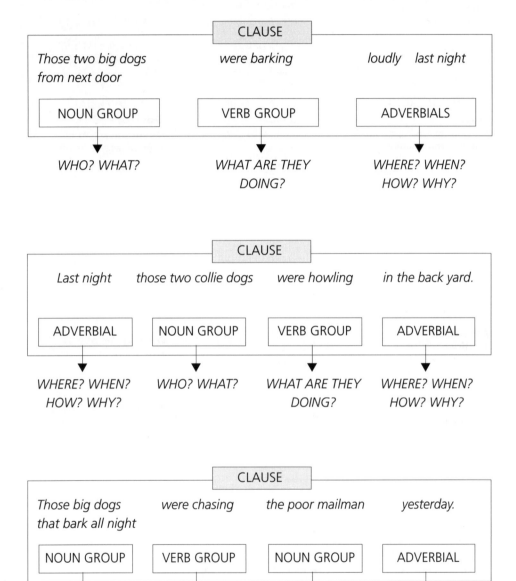

The table on the following page provides an overview of the grammatical features of English that we will now look at in turn.

Overview: Grammatical features of English

We can group the major grammatical categories in the clause into three major 'chunks': the noun group (including adjectivals), the verb group, and adverbials.

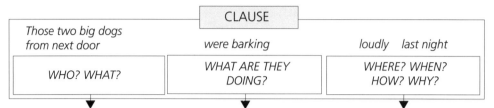

CLAUSE		
Those two big dogs from next door	*were barking*	*loudly* *last night*
WHO? WHAT?	WHAT ARE THEY DOING?	WHERE? WHEN? HOW? WHY?

NOUN GROUP

Nouns
- **living/non-living** *(bird/rock)*
- **human/non-human** *(baby/bird)*
- **masculine/feminine/neuter**
- **general/particular** *(cats/Kitty)*
- **concrete/abstract** *(clock/time)*
- **everyday/technical** *(food tube/oesophagus)*
- **objective/subjective** *(girl/flirt)*
- **countable/uncountable** *(biscuits/butter)*
- **common/proper** *(day/Friday)*
- **collective** *(flock; choir)*
- **singular/plural** *(child/children)*
- **compound nouns** *(surfboard)*

Adjectivals
- **articles** *(a/an, the)*
- **pointing words** *(this, those)*
- **possessives** *(their, Tom's)*
- **quantity adjectives** *(many, 3)*
- **opinion adjectives** *(sad, lovely)*
- **factual adjectives** *(big, old, red, square)*
- **comparing adjectives** *(more, bigger, best)*
- **classifiers** *(war plane)*
- **adjectival phrases*** *(the book on the top shelf) (people with curly hair)*
- **adjectival clauses** *(the boys sitting up the back) (the street where I live)*

(*including prepositions)

Pronouns
- **personal pronouns** *(I, us, her)*
- **possessive pronouns** *(hers, mine)*
- **relative pronouns** *(which, that)*
- **question pronouns** *(who? what?)*

VERB GROUP

Verb types
- **action verbs** *(Ben was wriggling)*
- **saying verbs** *(She murmured his name.)*
- **sensing verbs** thinking, feeling, perceiving *(She remembered him well.) (They will enjoy the concert.) (Cate heard nothing.)*
- **relating verbs** 'being and having' *(Frogs and toads are amphibians. Their mouths are large and they have small teeth.)*
- **existing verbs** *(There are some venomous frogs.)*

Tense
- **present** *(Koalas eat gumleaves.) (Kim is eating an icecream.)*
- **past** *(They ate slowly.) (They have eaten already.) (They were eating lunch.)*
- **future** *(I will eat later.) (I will be eating at home.)*
- **regular/irregular verbs**

Modals
- *(might, could, must)*

Negative forms
- *(didn't, doesn't)*

Multiword verbs
- *(began to cry; had a cry)*

ADVERBIALS

Adverbs and adverbial phrases
- **place** 'where?' *(away; to the shops)*
- **time** 'when?' *(lately; in the evening)*
- **manner** 'how?' quality *(sadly; with sorrow)* means *(by car; with a stick)* comparison *(differently; like a butterfly)*
- **cause** 'why?' *(due to ill-health; for his sanity)*
- **accompaniment** 'with whom?' *(together; with Grandma)*

Other types of adverbials
- **point of view, comment** *(in my opinion, personally, frankly, unfortunately)*
- **degree** *(more loudly; most loudly; extremely loudly; far, far away; almost too sweetly)*
- **modal adverbs** *(perhaps; maybe; definitely)*
- **focusing and emphasising** *(even; only)*

Noun groups

Noun groups provide information about the people, places, things and ideas which are involved in the clause.

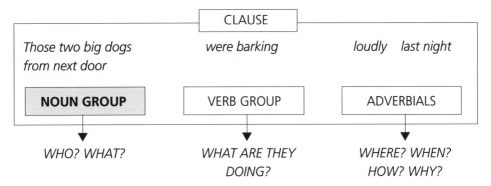

CLAUSE		
Those two big dogs from next door	*were barking*	*loudly last night*
NOUN GROUP	VERB GROUP	ADVERBIALS
↓	↓	↓
WHO? WHAT?	*WHAT ARE THEY DOING?*	*WHERE? WHEN? HOW? WHY?*

A noun group can consist simply of a noun (eg 'houses') or a pronoun (eg 'they'). Or it can be expanded to include very lengthy descriptions.

NOUN GROUP	VERB GROUP	NOUN GROUP
Mole and Ratty	were rowing	**the tiny wooden boat.**
They	noticed	**a handsome, dignified old house of mellowed brick, with well-kept lawns reaching down to the river's edge.**
It	was	**one of the nicest houses in these parts.**
The Rat	disembarked.	
Toad	had bought	**a shining new canary yellow gipsy caravan with red wheels.**

The grid on the following page outlines the main parts of the noun group. These are the resources which students can draw on when they are building up a description of something or someone. They are particularly important in text-types such as narratives (eg in setting the scene or describing a character) and information reports (eg in presenting information about a particular class of things).

NOUN GROUP									
ADJECTIVALS									NOUN
Article	Pointing word	Possessive	Quantity adjective	Opinion adjective	Factual adjective	Comparing adjective	Classifier	Noun or pronoun
								shoes
								they
		her		exquisite			dancing	shoes
some				smelly			running	shoes
			a hundred		black		school	shoes
			two	worn-out	old		walking	shoes
		Martin's		favourite			leather	shoes
	this				shiny		business	shoe
	those					more expensive	golf	shoes
the						most un-comfortable	tennis	shoe
WHICH?	WHICH?	WHOSE?	HOW MANY? HOW MUCH?	QUALITIES?	QUALITIES?	DEGREE?	WHAT TYPE?	WHO OR WHAT?

These groups are sometimes referred to as nominal groups or noun phrases. In functional grammar they are described in terms of participants in a process.

In this section we will look at the various parts of the noun group in detail: nouns, adjectivals and pronouns.

Nouns

A noun answers the question 'Who?' or 'What?'.

 Formation

Most nouns consist of a single meaningful unit (eg cat, nose, sock). Sometimes, however, we can form nouns by adding other meaningful units such as a suffix or another word.

Suffixes

We can form nouns by adding a suffix to a word such as a verb or an adjective, eg:

verb + –*ment*	→	astonish**ment**
verb + –*er/–or*	→	writ**er**, direct**or**
verb + –*ion*	→	distract**ion**
adjective + –*ness*	→	happi**ness**

Knowing a wide range of suffixes and prefixes can help readers to decipher unknown words and writers to extend their repertoire.

Singular/plural nouns

Nouns can refer to a single thing (singular) or a number of things (plural). In forming the plural, we generally add a suffix.

1. To make a noun plural, we generally add **–s** to the end of the noun (eg horse**s**, storey**s**, spa**s**)

2. If a noun ends in **–x, –s, –ss, –sh, –ch,** or **–z,** then we add **–es** (eg box**es**, bus**es**, loss**es**, brush**es**, branch**es**, quizz**es**)

3. When a noun ends in a consonant followed by **–y,** we form the plural with **–ies** (eg pon**ies**, stor**ies**)

4. Certain nouns which end in **–f** or **–fe** form their plural with **–ves** (eg hal**ves**, wi**ves**, kni**ves**) though others will simply take an **–s** (eg belief**s**, chief**s**, proof**s**, roof**s**)

5. Most nouns ending in **–o** add **–es** for the plural (eg potato**es**, hero**es**, mosquito**es**) but some (mainly abbreviated nouns) simply add **–s** (eg photo**s**, kilo**s**, video**s**, radio**s**, stereo**s**)

6. Some nouns from other languages have 'foreign' plurals (eg phenomenon → phenomen**a**; criterion → criteri**a**; nucleus → nucle**i**; referendum → referend**a**; analysis → analys**es**; vertebra → vertebr**ae**; formula → formul**ae**; appendix → append**ices**)

7. Some nouns change to a different form in the plural (eg children, women, mice)

8. Some nouns have the same form for both singular and plural (eg deer, sheep, aircraft, fruit, species)

9. Some nouns are always in the plural form (eg scissors, trousers, underpants, pliers, glasses). If we want to specify how many, we have to say, for example, 'three **pairs of** scissors'.

Collective nouns

Certain nouns refer to a group of people or things (eg family, choir, crew, bundle, council, enemy, herd, flock, a gaggle of geese, a pride of lions). Sometimes writers will create whimsical collective nouns, eg:

a cackle of hens
a clutch of handbags
a scuttle of meece

You can use either a singular or a plural verb after a collective noun. If you intend to refer to the group as a whole, you will use a singular verb (eg the choir **is** singing well). If you are referring more to the members of the group, you will use the plural form of the verb (eg the choir **are** going home early).

Compound nouns

In English we can increase our stock of vocabulary by combining two (or more) existing words to make a new word. A compound noun can consist of two nouns (eg horse thief, can opener, road works, law and order). They can also be formed by combining a noun and another word such as an adjective (eg natural resources, greenhouse, civil rights, social studies). Sometimes compound nouns are written as two separate words (eg human race) and sometimes they are joined with a hyphen (eg dry-cleaning) or even written as a single word (eg teabag)—especially if both the words are short.

Compound nouns which include a preposition make their plural by making the first noun plural (eg brothers-*in*-law, birds *of* prey, partners *in* crime)

Joining words to form compound nouns can lead to some creative combinations, such as the 'hippopotomouse', 'checkout chick', and 'shock jock'.

> ### The Jumboraffe
>
> If a giraffe wed an elephant
> And they had a jumbo son,
> Would he be tall, thin and spotty
> With ears that weighed a ton?
>
> *Bill Condon*

Creating new nouns

1. When we need a new noun in English, we often incorporate words or phrases from other languages, eg

   algebra (*an Arabic word*)
   billabong (*an Aboriginal word*)

2. If it is something technical, scientific or legal we often use words from Latin or ancient Greek (eg telephone, precedent). A knowledge of common Latin and Greek roots is useful in trying to work out the meaning of certain unfamiliar words, eg

   export
   autograph

3. Sometimes we take an old noun and use it with a different meaning (eg computer mouse) or we can take an adjective or verb and make it into a 'thing' (eg 'Red is my favourite colour', 'Walking is good for you').

   An attack of the **Lazies** is coming!
   I can feel them corroding my bones.
   They're eating up all of my energy beans
   And replacing my **yippees**! for groans.

   Bill Condon

4. Alternatively, we simply invent a noun, particularly in narratives and poetry. Edward Lear introduced us to 'the hills of the Chankly Bore' and 'the Jumblies', Pooh Bear is frightened of the 'heffalump', and Alice puzzled over 'Jabberwocks' and 'Bandersnatches'.

Nominalisation

One way of making a text more compact and 'written' is to change verbs (and other words) into nouns. Instead of saying, for example, 'When you heat a liquid it can change into a gas. When the gas cools it returns to a liquid.' we could use nominalisations: '**Vaporisation** is followed by **condensation**.'

Troubleshooting

As they enter later primary school, students will be encountering nominalisations in much of their reading. Because nominalisation tends to make texts dense and abstract many students will need assistance in learning how to 'unpack' this type of language.

Extended nouns

Sometimes a noun group can consist of two or more people, places or things (eg **Rachel and Kerry** didn't do their homework; **trains, planes and cars** are forms of transport; it's been used by every **Tom, Dick and Harry**.)

It is also possible to elaborate on a noun by restating it in another form (eg our dog **Harry**; London**, the capital of England**). These more complex forms are still noun groups.

 ### *Looking at meaning*

When we use language to represent our experience of the world, we use nouns (or 'naming words') to refer to people, places, things or concepts. Younger children will generally use nouns which are more concrete and everyday. As they get older however, they will also need to learn how to use nouns which are more abstract and technical.

We tend to organise our world into categories. When we talk about the meaning of nouns, we often refer to how they represent different aspects of our experience:

Living/non-living nouns

The world could be represented in terms of living things and non-living things. Certain learning areas tend to explore the world of living things (eg biology, botany, drama, literature, social studies) while others are more concerned with non-living things (eg physics, maths, astronomy, technology, geology).

Human/non-human nouns

Living things can be human or non-human. We are more likely to find human nouns in text-types such as narratives and recounts which deal with the actions, thoughts, feelings and sayings of people (or animals acting like people). Text-types such as information reports are more likely to include non-human nouns (eg bears, plants, marsupials).

Masculine/feminine/neuter

We also use language to divide the world into gender groups. We have masculine nouns referring to males (eg boy, father, uncle, Mr Smith, ram) and feminine nouns referring to females (eg girl, mother, aunt, Ms Jones, ewe). We even have neuter categories for those things which are of neither gender. This is an area which is currently the source of some dispute. Should we, for example, distinguish between people on the basis of their gender (hero/heroine; actor/actress)? Should we use masculine words (eg mankind, he) to refer to all humans? The way in which grammar is used to represent males and females (eg the gender balance in stories; what males do and what females do; which gender takes the initiating role in everyday activities) can be an interesting topic for a critical literacy session.

Proper/common nouns

Named people, places or things (eg Sarah, Mr Wang, Canberra, Holden) are called proper nouns. These begin with a capital letter. Other nouns are referred to as common nouns. We typically find proper nouns in text-types such as narratives, biographies, autobiographies, reports about countries, advertisements, and recounts.

Particular/general nouns

When we are dealing with familiar, personal experiences, we tend to use nouns which refer to particular people, places and things (eg mum, the lady next door, my doll, our house, this ant). These are often found in recounts of personal experience, stories, and descriptions. As they progress through school, however, students need to be able to move from the particular to the general, referring to classes of things rather than a particular individual (eg **transport** as opposed to 'our station wagon'; **domestic animals** as opposed to 'Toby'; **community workers** as opposed to 'Mrs Thomas'; **mountain ranges** as opposed to 'Mt Keira'). General nouns are more likely to be found in text types such as information reports and explanations.

Everyday/technical nouns

When students are learning about concepts which are specific to a certain field of study, they need to use technical terminology which is precise and unambiguous (eg digit, sonnet, vertebrate, rectangle, carbon dioxide, secondary sources, action verb). A technical noun is one which has been tightly defined within a particular discipline so that people working within that discipline can share knowledge efficiently and precisely. As students become apprenticed into the specialist disciplines of later primary and secondary education, they must learn the technical language of those areas.

Concrete/abstract nouns

Another important shift in students' learning is from the concrete to the abstract. Concrete nouns refer to those things which are physical, material, tangible (eg table, apple, body, dirt, building). When we refer to things such as ideas or concepts or feelings which cannot be touched or seen, we use abstract nouns (eg memory, honesty, multiplication, sadness, hypothesis, democracy).

Countable/uncountable nouns

Certain nouns refer to things which are able to be counted (eg ten apples, a couple of books, several nuns). Some nouns, however, refer to things which are seen as an uncountable mass (eg air, intelligence, research, information, water, happiness, respect, snow, advice, furniture, hair, homework, traffic, politics). Uncountable nouns generally represent qualities, substances, and abstract notions.

Some nouns can be both countable and uncountable (eg ten cakes/some cake; Australian wines/a sip of wine).

Troubleshooting

Students can experience problems when talking about amounts in relation to countable and uncountable nouns; for example, the difference between 'eat **less** butter' (uncountable) and 'eat **fewer** chips' (countable); or between 'there's not **much** traffic' (uncountable) and 'there aren't **many** cars' (countable).

Uncountable nouns can often cause difficulties for ESL students who might use them in the plural (eg 'We don't have a lot of informations').

Metaphorical nouns

Sometimes we represent one thing by referring to it metaphorically as something else (eg referring to a thing as if it had human qualities, as with personification). This is one way of extending and enriching meaning and of creating unexpected and often incongruent meanings.

The Beach

The beach is a quarter of golden fruit,
a soft ripe melon
sliced to a half-moon curve,
having a thick green rind
of jungle growth;
and the sea devours it
with its sharp,
sharp white teeth.

William Hart-Smith

Apart from representing our experience of the world, nouns can be used in interpersonal ways to express judgements, to assign roles and to create relationships.

Objective/subjective nouns

In using nouns, we can be objective and impartial, or we can be more subjective and judgemental. Students need to be able to identify when a text is attempting to persuade them to a particular point of view. This often happens through the choice of nouns made by the speaker or writer (eg obsession, mongrel, eyesore, monstrosity, cult). Subjective nouns are often found in text-types which seek to influence (eg exposition, advertisements, editorials, stories).

'Point of view' nouns

In certain contexts, words which sound quite objective can be selected to represent the world in a certain way and to present a particular point of view (eg bureaucrat, evidence, crime, victim, resort, problem, hero, man-in-the-street). Whereas a police report might represent an incident as a 'home invasion and robbery involving three criminals', the participants might see it as 'doing a job with my mates to get some money'.

Terms of address

When we are talking with someone, we often use terms of address which indicate our relationship to that person or which position them in a particular role. These are generally nouns such as titles, nicknames, terms of endearment, or proper names (eg 'Hello **Mrs McNaught**', 'Come here, **Tommy**', 'Yes **sir**', 'G'day **Jacko**', 'Okay **darling**', 'Certainly **Your Worship**'). These are sometimes called vocatives. Terms of address are a significant resource for developing relationships in terms of power, status, familiarity, and feelings. Look how carefully Kipling uses terms of address to define roles and relationships in the *Just So Stories*: the independent Cat addresses the human as 'O my Enemy and Wife of my Enemy' while the more submissive Bat calls her 'Oh my Hostess and wife of my Host' and the tamed horse now refers to her as 'O my Mistress and Wife of my Master'. Kipling himself directly engages with his child-reader by using the term of endearment 'Best Beloved'.

Summary: Nouns in a text

Look at the different kinds of meanings being created through the nouns in the following texts:

Text 1: Narrative text

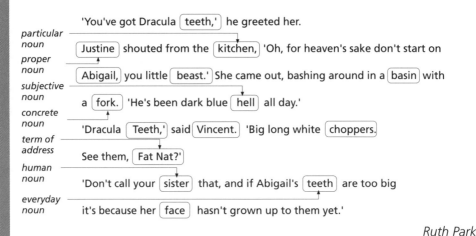

particular noun
proper noun
subjective noun
concrete noun
term of address
human noun
everyday noun

'You've got Dracula teeth,' he greeted her.

Justine shouted from the kitchen, 'Oh, for heaven's sake don't start on

Abigail, you little beast.' She came out, bashing around in a basin with

a fork. 'He's been dark blue hell all day.'

'Dracula Teeth,' said Vincent. 'Big long white choppers.

See them, Fat Nat?'

'Don't call your sister that, and if Abigail's teeth are too big

it's because her face hasn't grown up to them yet.'

Ruth Park

Text 2: Explanation

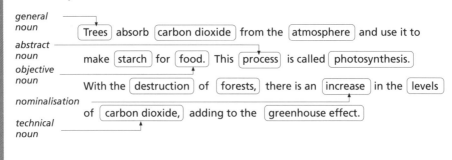

general noun
abstract noun
objective noun
nominalisation
technical noun

Trees absorb carbon dioxide from the atmosphere and use it to

make starch for food. This process is called photosynthesis.

With the destruction of forests, there is an increase in the levels

of carbon dioxide, adding to the greenhouse effect.

In Text 1, the nouns are involved in constructing a familiar world of concrete, particular, everyday things such as the kitchen, a basin and a fork, inhabited by people with names. This world has interpersonal dimensions through the choice of subjective nouns such as 'beast' and 'choppers' as well as the way in which the participants address each other: 'you little beast', 'Fat Nat'.

In Text 2, the world being constructed is much more objective. Rather than particular individuals, it is concerned with generalisations ('trees' in general). It deals with technical entities from the discipline of science ('carbon dioxide', 'photosynthesis'). It involves abstractions ('process') and nominalised phenomena ('increase').

Nouns: Development through the stages

Early Primary

Learning to ...

Most students should be able to use an increasing range of nouns to refer to people, places and things in their home, school and community environments. These nouns will be primarily everyday, concrete and particular, though generalised nouns and categories will become more evident, particularly with teacher guidance and selection of more general themes and topics.

Learning about ...

In their discussions, writing, reading and viewing, terms such as 'name', 'naming word', or 'label' could be introduced. They should be able to recognise and talk about nouns of various types where appropriate (eg proper/common; living/non-living; human/non-human). They should know to use capitals for proper nouns and how to form the plural of common, regular nouns.

Mid Primary

Learning to ...

Most students should be employing a wide variety of nouns. They should be developing the ability to use synonyms, using two or more nouns to refer to the same thing (eg puss, kitty, cat, feline). While many of these nouns will be learnt through conversation, classroom discussion and reading, there is scope for new nouns to be introduced more explicitly through work on topics and themes, particularly more abstract and technical nouns.

Learning about ...

In their discussions, writing, reading and viewing, they should be able to recognise and talk about how certain types of nouns can be used to bias a text or influence the listener/speaker (eg subjective nouns, terms of address, masculine/feminine/neuter nouns). By now, students should be using the term 'noun' and they should be able to identify various types of nouns (eg singular/plural, collective, compound) and to form the plural of many irregular nouns. They should be able to identify how nouns can be formed by using prefixes and suffixes.

Later Primary

Learning to ...

Most students should be understanding and employing a wide variety of nouns to refer to the people, objects, places and concepts in each of the subject areas. They should be able to select those nouns which are most appropriate to express an idea involving fine distinctions and detail. In factual texts they should be comprehending and using general, abstract and technical nouns (and defining the latter where appropriate). In literary texts they should be appreciating and attempting to use nouns which best capture the character, mood, setting, and so on.

Learning about ...

Students should be able to reflect on and discuss the selection of different types of nouns in texts they are reading and writing and how well they serve their purpose in terms of representing particular ideas, influencing listeners/readers, or establishing relationships. They should be able to identify abstract and technical nouns. They should be able to form the plural of most commonly encountered irregular plurals of nouns. If seen as useful, students could be introduced to 'countable' and 'uncountable' nouns and 'extended' nouns. They should be familiar with a number of common Latin and Greek roots and could explore the origins and history of particular nouns.

Adjectivals

Adjectivals play a major role in building up the information around a noun. They provide many different types of information:

- which specific thing is being referred to?
- who does it belong to?
- how many things are involved?
- what is the speaker's opinion about this thing?
- what attributes does it have? (eg size, shape, colour, size)
- how does it compare with other things?
- what class does it belong to?

Generally adjectivals are included within the noun group, though they can also be used after a relating verb, eg She is **tired**. (See the section on relating verbs, p.59.)

The term 'adjectivals' is used here to refer to various types of words which provide information about the noun. Teachers may use their own judgement as to whether it is useful to use this term with students, or to use a less technical term such as 'describers' or 'noun describers'. Sometimes it will be quite appropriate to simply use 'adjective' when referring to the different types of adjectives. However, this term is not accurate when talking about other components of the noun group such as articles, demonstratives, possessives, adjectival phrases and adjectival clauses.

Adjectivals fall into two main groups:

- those words which answer the question 'which?' or 'whose?'. (The technical term for these words is **determiners**, but students need not be expected to know this.)
- those words which answer such questions as 'how many?', 'what like?', 'what type?'. These are different types of **adjectives**.

Primary age students are not necessarily expected to recognise the difference between determiners and adjectives. It is more important that they simply realise that there are a number of different types of words which describe nouns as shown on the following page.

The following sections will examine the function and formation of the different types of words which describe nouns.

ADJECTIVALS (noun describers)								
DETERMINERS			ADJECTIVES					NOUN
Article	Pointing word	Possessive	Quantity adjective	Opinion adjective	Factual adjective	Comparing adjective	Classifying adjective	Noun or pronoun
eg a/an some the	eg this that these those	eg my his their your Diana's	eg two a dozen third	eg elegant grotty poor scary difficult	eg blue round big thin soft	eg smoother more pretty the worst	eg African plastic	shoes geese Maria sunspot Islam nucleus meaning
WHICH?	WHICH?	WHOSE?	HOW MANY? HOW MUCH?	QUALITIES?	QUALITIES?	DEGREE?	WHAT TYPE?	WHO OR WHAT?

Articles

Articles answer the question 'which one?'

The articles in English are used to give an indication about the degree to which a reference to something is general or specific. If it is a general reference, we use the **indefinite article**—**a** or **an** (eg We saw **a** whale). If it is specific we use the **definite article**—**the** (eg **The** whale plunged into the water).

🔲 Formation

The indefinite article is usually **a**, but it changes to **an** in front of a word beginning with a vowel sound (eg **an** elephant) or a silent 'h' (eg **an** hour). In the plural, we might use no article (Movies are expensive.) or a word like **some** (**Some** movies are expensive.).

The definite article has only one form: **the**. It is used in front of both singular and plural nouns (eg **the** boy/**the** boys).

👁 Looking at meaning

The indefinite article can be used when we want to make a reference somewhat vague (eg We went to see **a** movie.).

We use the definite article, **the**, when we have already generally introduced the thing we are talking about and now want to refer to it more specifically. (eg He found himself rolling in the warm grass of **a** great meadow. … He pursued his way across **the** meadow.) The use of articles forms links within a text. (See p.108 for further information on how articles contribute to the cohesion of texts.)

Often we don't have to introduce the thing to our listener or reader because we can assume that they would realise what we meant from the context (eg **The** sun was shining in **the** clear blue sky as Jenny left the house.)

Troubleshooting

*Generally the use of the articles is relatively straightforward and should not cause problems for students. It is the sort of knowledge which we pick up from immersion in the language and use without thinking. Students learning English as a second language (ESL), however, particularly those more recently arrived, could have difficulties knowing when to use **a/an**, when to use **the**, and when not to use anything. Look, for example, at how in English we can refer to a general class of things (eg in an information report):*

> **The whale** *is a mammal. (definite article)*
> **Whales** *are mammals. (no article)*
> **A whale** *is a mammal. (indefinite article)*

Many languages use articles in quite different ways, so some ESL students will need assistance in this area.

Pointing words

Pointing words answer the question 'which one/s?'

 Formation

There are only four main pointing words in English:

	near	far
SINGULAR	**this**	**that**
PLURAL	**these**	**those**

In many grammars, these are referred to as **demonstratives**.

 Looking at meaning

Pointing adjectives tell us which specific thing is being referred to in terms of its distance in space and time. Is it the one close by (eg **this** apple/**these** apples)? Or is it further away (eg **that** apple/**those** apples)?

> Do you want **this** newspaper or **that** one?
> **These** batteries don't work.
> **These** days it's hard to find work.
> Watch out for **that** step.
> How much are **those** sneakers?

Sometimes pointing adjectives can be used when we want to be more specific or more emphatic:

> Give me **that** book with the torn cover.
> **That** sort of behaviour is unacceptable.

Pointing adjectivals held to establish 'point of view', locating the speaker in relation to other people or things in the environment.

> **This** little piggy went to market,
> **This** little piggy stayed home,
> **This** little piggy had roast beef,
> **This** little piggy had none,
> And **this** little piggy went wee-wee-wee-wee all the way home.
> *Nursery Rhyme*

Possessives

Possessives answer the question 'who owns it?'

Formation

There are two types of possessives: possessive determiners (my, your, his, her, its, our, and their) and possessive adjectives (Sandy's, my mother's). Here we will group them together and simply call them 'possessives'.

The following rules show how possessives are formed:

1. To make a singular noun possessive, add **'s**:
   eg a dog**'s** life; Brooke**'s** bag; the boy**'s** leg
2. If the noun ends in s, you can simply put an apostrophe:
   eg Jame**s'** car (though sometimes this is written as James**'s** car)
3. If the noun is plural, put an apostrophe after the **s**:
   eg the bird**s'** nests, the student**s'** lunches
4. If the plural is an irregular one (and does not end in s) add **'s**:
   eg the women**'s** toilets, some children**'s** hair

A good rule of thumb is: Add 's to any noun to make it possessive, but if it already ends in s, simply add an apostrophe after the s.

Troubleshooting

Note that **it's** is the contraction of it is—not the possessive form (**its**):

> **It's** quiet. (It is quiet.)
> The dog ate **its** dinner.

This is a common misunderstanding. Students in each stage might need to be reminded of this difference. It can be pointed out, for example, when doing guided reading with a book such as Caterpillar Diary:

> *This caterpillar has shed **its** skin. Now **it's** green and it has grown a lot bigger. ...*
> *Last night my moth came out of **its** cocoon. I know **it's** a moth because **its** feelers*
> *are shaped like feathers.*

👁 *Looking at meaning*

This is My Chair

This is **my** chair.
Go away and sit somewhere else.
This one is all **my** own.
It is the only thing in your house that I possess
And insist upon possessing.
Everything else therein is **yours**.
My dish,
My toys,
My basket,
My scratching post and **my** Ping-Pong ball;
You provided them for me.
This chair I selected for myself.
I like it,
It suits me.
You have the sofa,
The stuffed chair
And the footstool.
I don't go and sit on them do I?
Then why cannot you leave me **mine**,
And let us have no further argument?

Paul Gallico

Notice how possessives are used here to highlight the notion of ownership. The cat's world is carefully divided into 'mine' and 'yours', but even then it distinguishes between the possessions which have been given to it and the one possession it chose for itself. This poem could be used as a stimulus for a discussion on the nature of possessions and ownership (including the ownership of pets)— and how these might differ from culture to culture.

Quantity adjectives

Quantity adjectives tell us about 'how many'/'how much' and 'in which order'. These are sometimes referred to as quantifiers or quantitative/numerative adjectives.

👁 *Looking at meaning*

There are two main types of quantity adjectives: cardinal and ordinal.

- Cardinal refers to the quantity of things:
  three bags full, **four** little ducks, my **two** sons, a **hundred** eyes

- Ordinal refers to the order:
  the **first** time, the **third** place-getter, the **fifth** amendment

These quantity adjectives are often found in maths problems and procedures.

> **Five** little rabbits sat under a tree
> The **first** one said, "What can I see?"
> The **second** one said, "A man with a gun"
> The **third** one said, "Quick, let's run"
> The **fourth** one said, "Let's hide in the shade"
> The **fifth** one said, "I'm not afraid".
> "Bang!" went the gun and missed every one.
>
> *Understanding Mathematics*
>
> **Ten** fat sausages sizzling in a pan.
> **Ten** fat sausages sizzling in a pan.
> **One** went pop and **one** went bang.
> That left **eight** fat sausages sizzling in the pan ...
>
> *Understanding Mathematics*

Apart from these precise references to numbers, we can also have more vague references to quantities and amounts:

most of the boys
many babies
a few dollars
several reasons
too **much** cake

Sometimes it is important to be precise (eg in providing statistical evidence for an argument or in a maths problem). At other times, we might want to use more indefinite terms. These are often found in information reports (eg **Most** herbivores ..., but **a few** ...) and in expositions (**The great majority of** scientists agree ...). These adjectivals can be arranged in a continuum, eg:

none of ➤ hardly any ➤ a few ➤ some ➤ a good number of ➤ many ➤ most ➤ nearly all ➤ all

Here are some quantity adjectives. (Some of them can go in front of a determiner, in which case they are called 'pre-determiners', eg **some of** <u>the</u> trees, **all** <u>his</u> dinner.)

a lot of	a little	no	a bag of	enough
all	both	a bit of	each	every
several	much	plenty of	numerous	various
more	few	less	many	
some	any	another	a great deal of	

Opinion adjectives

Opinion adjectives give the writer's or speaker's evaluation of the thing in question.

 Formation

Opinion adjectives can be formed by adding suffixes to a word such as a noun or verb, eg:

noun + –*ful*	→	wonder**ful**
noun + –*y*	→	funn**y**
noun + –*ish*	→	ghoul**ish**
noun + –*able/–ible*	→	respect**able**
noun + –*ous*	→	marvell**ous**
verb + –*ing*	→	frighten**ing**
verb + –*ed*	→	embarrass**ed**

Note that sometimes the final consonant is doubled before adding the suffix (eg fun → funny). Prefixes can change the meaning of the adjective, eg **un**funny, **dis**believing.

We can sometimes find compound opinion adjectives such as 'wishy-washy'.

When regular words do not quite capture the meaning, learners can create original opinion adjectives in the tradition of Kipling (describing a cub as 'little and **fubsy**'), Lear ('Below her home the river rolled with soft **meloobious** sound'), and A.A. Milne (who told of Pooh's '**goloptious** full-up pot of honey').

I was once a Bottle of Ink,
Inky
Dinky
Thinky
Inky
Blacky Minky
Bottle of ink!

> **P** was once a little Pump,
> **Pumpy**
> **Slumpy**
> **Flumpy**
> **Pumpy**
> **Dumpy, Thumpy**
> Little Pump!

Edward Lear

👁 *Looking at meaning*

If we want to express our judgement about something, we can use an adjective which indicates an opinion. While most other adjectives are used to build up a picture of the world, opinion adjectives have a more interpersonal function, expressing a particular point of view. When we give our opinion, we are creating a situation where our listener or reader will probably react, either agreeing with our evaluation or taking issue with it. The opinion adjective invites us not simply to observe but to interact.

This type of adjective is important in critical reading activities, where students need to identify how, for example, a newspaper article or magazine story or television documentary is influencing them to see things in a particular way.

In their own writing, students need to extend their repertoire of opinion adjectives so that they are able to express their evaluation of things, people and situations in less clichéd, more subtle and convincing ways (eg in stories, recounts, biographies, and expositions). This type of adjective is generally not used in text-types such as information reports and explanations.

These adjectives can often be arranged along a continuum, eg:

deadly dull → boring → so so → mildly interesting → fascinating

Students could also look for synonyms (hot/scorching/blistering/sizzling) and antonyms (sizzling/chilly) in extending their pool of opinion adjectives.

And of course they can make up their own as Lewis Carroll did:

> 'Twas brillig, and the **slithy** toves
> Did gyre and gimble in the wabe;
> All **mimsy** were the borogoves,
> And the **mome** raths outgrabe.

Lewis Carroll

We could also include here a group called 'emphasising adjectives' which are used when we want to emphasise our opinions about something (eg a **complete** fool, an **utter** disaster, an **absolute** scandal).

Factual adjectives

Factual adjectives describe something in an objective way, giving information about attributes which can be verified, measured, and agreed upon as true.

 **Formation**

Factual adjectives are formed in similar ways to opinion adjectives.

Subtle differences in meaning can be created by using suffixes such as '-ish' (eg yellowish, squarish).

Again we can have compound factual adjectives: 'Next they met a **long-necked, long-legged, sharp-clawed** emu.'

Looking at meaning

Factual adjectives provide objective information about something. They describe the attributes which a thing possesses: its size, age, shape, colour, and other qualities. These adjectives are found in most text-types, but particularly in information reports, descriptions and procedures.

> Blue heelers have a **thickset** body with **pricked** ears. They have a **smooth, mottled-blue** coat and a **red** or **black** face with a **dark, round** spot over each eye.

While most adjectives provide a description which is everyday and concrete, it is possible to find adjectives which are more technical and/or abstract:

nutritious foods
a **contagious** disease
nitrogen-rich soil
a **reasonable** suggestion
the **subtle** differences
a **critical** review

Most opinion adjectives and factual adjectives can be modified by certain adverbs which tell us the degree of intensity:

the **extremely** sad death
a **very** old book
a **somewhat** odd story
a **slightly** different way
a **rather** long movie

We can also intensify a description by repeating the adjective:

'Oh, you **wicked wicked** little thing!' cried Alice.
He was an **old old** dog.

Comparing adjectives

Comparing adjectives tell us the relative amount of a quality. Comparing adjectives are often referred to as comparatives (eg smarter) or superlatives (eg the smartest).

🔲 *Formation*

Most opinion adjectives and factual adjectives can be used in a comparative way. To make a comparative or superlative, you add **–er** or **–est** to the adjective:

long	➤	longer/longest
sad	➤	sadder/saddest

Note that when **–er** and **–est** are added to some endings, there is a spelling change (eg a final single consonant following a single vowel is doubled (sli**mm**er) before adding the comparative endings).

If the adjective has two syllables or more, then the words **more** and **most** are used with the adjective rather than adding the endings **–er** and **–est**:

complicated	➤	more complicated/most complicated

Of course, rules can be broken for effect:

> The horriblest teacher I ever knew
> Was Mr Ratface Pettigrew.
> *Bill Condon*

There are some two syllable adjectives which can take either form of comparison:

happy	➤	happier/happiest	*or*	more happy/most happy
common	➤	commoner/commonest	*or*	more common/most common

We can also compare something in terms of what it is **less** than:

complicated	➤	**less** complicated/**least** complicated

We can also compare it to something that is the same, or similar:

complicated	➤	**as** complicated **as**

Some adjectives have irregular comparative forms:

bad	➤	worse/worst
good	➤	better/best

👁 *Looking at meaning*

Comparing adjectives are often found in text-types such as information reports which compare and contrast different types of things (eg frogs and toads) and in descriptions and narratives where people, places and things are being compared.

If Rabbit
Was **bigger**
And **fatter**
And **stronger**,
Or **bigger**
Than Tigger,
If Tigger was **smaller**,
Then Tigger's bad habit
Of bouncing at Rabbit
Would matter no longer,
If Rabbit
Was **taller**.

A.A. Milne

The **most attractive**
female I've
ever met was
an African lioness
called Elsa.
She seemed
most beautiful
of all, when she
turned her back!

Godfrey Winn

Classifying adjectives

Classifying adjectives are used to place something into a particular group: 'what type?'.

 **Formation**

Classifying adjectives often look like factual adjectives and can be formed in the same way.

Many classifiers are actually nouns being used with the function of classifying:

> **animal** doctor
> **science** lesson
> **passenger** train

Sometimes a classifier can be a verb:

> **washing** machine
> **boiled** water

For this reason, it might be better to refer to this group as **classifiers** rather than 'classifying adjectives'.

It is possible to have compound classifiers:

> He's not a **sit-by-the-fire-and-purr** cat,
> A **look-at-my-exquisite-fur** cat,
> No, he's not! ...
> He's a fat cat, a rat cat,
> A "**what on earth was that**?" cat.
> *Gina Wilson*

… and even to create new classifiers, as in Edward Lear's '4 gallons of clarified **crumbobblious** sauce'.

👁 *Looking at meaning*

Classifiers tell us which class the thing belongs to. We could, for example, divide newspapers into different classes: daily or weekly; tabloid or broadsheet. Or we could talk about different types of politicians: female or male; conservative or progressive; Labor or Liberal.

Classifying adjectives are important in text-types such as information reports. They are one of the resources we use to categorise the world in various ways (eg venomous snakes/non-venomous snakes; igneous rocks/sedimentary rocks/ metamorphic rocks).

Adjectives which indicate nationality, location or origin are usually classifiers:

Australian history
a **British** passport
the **southern** lakes
a **medieval** village

Words which refer to the material that something is made out of are generally classifiers:

a **cotton** dress
leather boots
a **plastic** bucket
a **clay brick** house

Troubleshooting

Sometimes it is difficult to tell the difference between factual adjectives and classifiers. Here's a tip:

> *If a word is a classifier, it cannot take an intensifier such as 'very' or 'rather'. You couldn't say, for example, 'a very science lesson' or 'a rather passenger train'. It also can't be used in the comparative. You couldn't say 'a bricker wall' or 'the most Hereford cow'.*

Adding more information to the noun

So far we have looked at how we can build up information about something by adding different types of adjectivals in front of the noun. We can also use adjectivals to add further information after the noun. This can take the form of an adjectival phrase, eg:

a nice little nose **with freckles on it**

or an adjectival clause, eg:

the umbrella **that Peter lent me yesterday**

These answer the question 'Which?' and are often found in text-types such as stories and information reports where additional information is needed about something. They are sometimes referred to as embedded phrases/clauses, qualifiers or post-modifiers.

Adjectival phrases

NOUN GROUP		
	NOUN	ADJECTIVAL PHRASE
the most famous	books	**of ancient China**
those silly	girls	**without raincoats**
the traditional	dress	**for Japanese men**

🔁 *Formation*

An adjectival phrase is a noun group preceded by a preposition, eg:

PREPOSITION	NOUN GROUP
in	the next room
beside	the bed
from	next door
with	the dirty old jeans

This is sometimes called a prepositional phrase because it begins with a preposition. There are, however, different types of prepositional phrases which do different jobs. In this case, the prepositional phrase is doing the job of providing information about a noun, so we call it an adjectival phrase. It becomes part of the larger noun group:

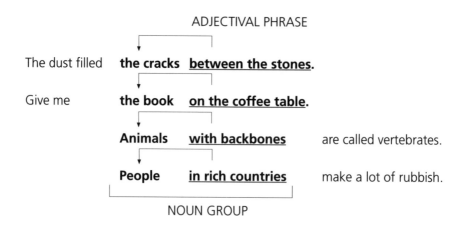

ADJECTIVAL PHRASE

The dust filled **the cracks** **between the stones.**

Give me **the book** **on the coffee table.**

Animals **with backbones** are called vertebrates.

People **in rich countries** make a lot of rubbish.

NOUN GROUP

Looking at meaning

We can specify which thing we are referring to by adding an adjectival phrase.
Adjectival phrases give information in answer to questions such as:

where?	a partridge **in a pear tree**
with what?	a big hollow log **with a lot of holes in it**
what like?	with hair **like a Persian cat in a power point**
whose?	the tomb **of Pharaoh Tutankhamen**
about what?	rumours **about his death**
what kind?	gifts **of diamonds and rubies**
why?	a cure **for cancer**

Adjectival clauses

NOUN GROUP		
	NOUN	**ADJECTIVAL CLAUSE**
an old	lady	**who swallowed a fly**
the	person	**to whom I am writing**
the unfortunate	woman	**whose credit card was stolen**
the ancient	bones	**that archaeologists have found**
the	house	**which Jack built**
the historic	town	**where Lincoln was born**
the	part	**I like best**

Like adjectival phrases, adjectival clauses provide extra information about the
noun. An adjectival clause identifies which thing we are referring to.

🔲 *Formation*

Unlike adjectival phrases, adjectival clauses contain a verb:

the people **who <u>fought</u> for freedom**
the tree **under which they <u>were dancing</u>**
the ships **that <u>carry</u> these containers**
colonists **<u>looking</u> for gold**
a dog **<u>riddled</u> with fleas**
the first Europeans **<u>to settle</u> in North America**

Sometimes a full verb isn't used:

the train **<u>coming</u> around the bend** ...
the people **<u>killed</u> by the hurricane** ...
the desire **<u>to win</u>** ...
one way **of <u>passing</u> the time** ...

They often begin with a relative pronoun (eg **who, whom, whose, which, that,** and **where**) which refers to the preceding noun group, eg:

the <u>place</u> **where** I was born

> This is the Farmer **that** sowed the corn,
> **That** fed the cock **that** crowed in the morn,
> **That** waked the priest all shaven and shorn,
> **That** married the man all tattered and torn,
> **That** kissed the maiden all forlorn,
> **That** milked the cow with the crumpled horn,
> **That** tossed the dog,
> **That** worried the cat,
> **That** killed the rat, **that** ate the malt,
> **That** lay in the house **that** Jack built.

They are therefore sometimes called relative clauses. In some cases, however, the relative pronoun is omitted, eg:

the coat **(that) I'm wearing** ...

We can also see adjectival clauses as part of the noun group:

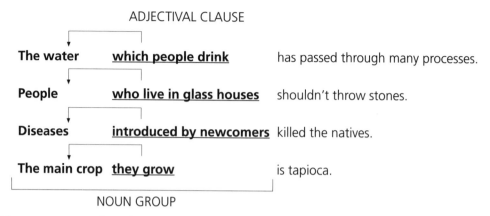

ADJECTIVAL CLAUSE

The water **which people drink** has passed through many processes.

People **who live in glass houses** shouldn't throw stones.

Diseases **introduced by newcomers** killed the natives.

The main crop **they grow** is tapioca.

NOUN GROUP

This is one way of combining pieces of information into a single unit, rather than a series of separate clauses or sentences.

Newcomers introduced diseases.
These diseases killed the natives.

↓

Diseases introduced by newcomers killed the natives.

Looking at meaning

This more complex use of language is regarded as more mature and concise and should be encouraged in older students' writing.

Some students may have trouble reading texts which contain these structures. In this case, it is often useful to demonstrate how to 'unpack' the noun group:

Musical instruments **that are played by hitting or shaking** belong to the percussion group.

↓

Some instruments are played by hitting (eg a drum)
Some instruments are played by shaking (eg a tambourine)
These instruments belong to the percussion group.

Summary: Adjectivals in a text

The following extract from *The Loaded Dog* by Henry Lawson demonstrates how a variety of adjectivals can contribute to building up the description of the dog.

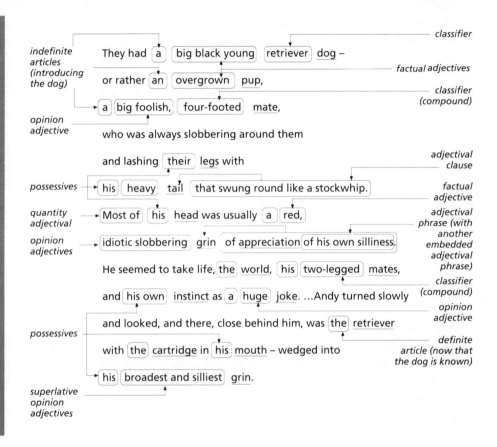

This text contains a number of lengthy noun groups, typical of descriptive and informative texts:

a big black young retriever dog
an overgrown pup
a big foolish, four-footed mate
his heavy tail that swung round like a stockwhip
most of his head
a red, idiotic slobbering grin of appreciation of his own silliness
life, the world, his two-legged mates, and his own instinct (extended noun group)
his broadest and silliest grin

Early Primary

Learning to ...

Most students should be able to use a range of adjectivals to describe people, places and things in their home, school and community environments. Their writing may contain simple noun groups which include articles, possessives, factual adjectives (eg size, shape, colour) and common opinion adjectives (eg 'nice', 'kind'). Teachers can foster an increase in the detail of the descriptive resources (eg not just 'big' but synonyms such as 'huge', 'enormous', 'immense').

Learning about ...

In their discussions, writing, reading and viewing, they should be able to recognise words (and visuals) which provide a description. In these discussions, terms such as 'describing words' could be introduced. They should be able to recognise and talk about simple adjectivals of various types where appropriate (eg 'quantity', 'opinion', 'factual'). Over time, students could be introduced to the term 'adjective' or 'adjectival' (although explanations such as 'words which tell you how many', 'words which give your opinion' or 'describing words which give you factual information' may be more appropriate at this stage).

Mid Primary

Learning to ...

Most students should be employing a wide variety of adjectivals. They should be moving beyond the more clichéd describing words (eg 'good', 'lovely', 'nice'). While many of these adjectivals will be learnt through conversation and reading, there is scope for more uncommon and challenging adjectivals to be introduced more explicitly through work on topics and themes. Various intensifiers might be modelled (eg 'very calm', 'extremely rude', 'incredibly brave').

Learning about ...

By now, students should be learning to name the different types of adjectivals encountered and to understand how these help to build up information about the noun in the noun group. Students should be able to differentiate between 'opinion' and 'factual' adjectives and to talk about how certain types of opinion adjectives can be used to influence the listener/speaker. They should be able to identify various types of adjectivals (eg pointing, possessive and comparing). They should know how comparing adjectives are formed, particularly the common irregular ones. They need to know how to form the possessive (eg John's, mothers', its). They should be able to recognise how adjectivals can be formed by using prefixes and suffixes. Some students might benefit from understanding the difference between the pointing words 'this' and 'that', 'these' and 'those'. Most students will not need much explicit discussion of articles (except for using 'an' before a vowel), but some ESL students might experience difficulties with these.

Later primary

Learning to ...

Most students should be understanding and employing a wide variety of adjectivals to describe the people, objects, places and concepts in each of the subject areas. They should be able to select those adjectivals which are most appropriate to express fine distinctions and detail. In factual texts they should be comprehending and using abstract and technical adjectivals (and defining the latter where appropriate). In literary texts they should be appreciating and attempting to use adjectivals which best develop the character, mood, setting, image, and so on. They should be comprehending and constructing detailed noun groups which include a range of adjectivals, including adjectival phrases and adjectival clauses.

Learning about ...

Students should be able to reflect on and discuss the selection of different types of adjectivals in texts they are reading and writing and how well they serve their purpose in terms of creating an image, influencing the listener/reader, adding precision, and so on. They should be able to identify factual adjectivals which are abstract or technical. They should be able to recognise the function of classifying adjectives (eg in information reports). Some students will benefit from knowing how adjectival phrases and adjectival clauses can build up information in the noun group. If seen as useful, students could be introduced to 'cardinal' and 'ordinal' quantity adjectives. They should be familiar with a number of common Latin and Greek roots relating to certain adjectivals.

Pronouns

Instead of constantly repeating a noun group, we can replace it with a pronoun:

> The old woman sat down wearily. **She** was tired from walking so far.
> Bob looked at the little brown puppy. **It** was shivering.

The main types of pronouns are personal, possessive, relative, and interrogative.

Personal pronouns

 Formation

	SINGULAR		PLURAL	
	SUBJECT	OBJECT	SUBJECT	OBJECT
1st person (*'speaking'*)	I	me	we	us
2nd person (*'spoken to'*)	you	you	you	you
3rd person (*'spoken of'*)	he she it	him her it	they	them

Personal pronouns are used to refer to the person who is speaking (the 'first' person), the person being spoken to (the 'second' person), or the person/thing being spoken about (the 'third' person).

They can refer to one person or thing (singular) or more than one (plural).

They can also be (i) the **subject** of the **verb** (eg the person doing the action)

SUBJECT PRONOUN	
I	*heard* the news yesterday.
We	*wanted to come* with you.
You	*should have told* Mrs Peters.
He	*was* in the bathroom.
She	*spoke* very slowly.
It	*refused to budge.*
They	*opened* it carefully.

or (ii) the **object** of the **verb** (eg the person receiving the action)

	OBJECT OF VERB	
Susan *told*	**me**	the whole story.
He *gave*	**us**	the key.
Cigarettes *will kill*	**you**	
The guards *dragged*	**him**	from the building.
They *transferred*	**her**	to intensive care.
Then *place*	**it**	in the cold water.
You *can see*	**them**	through the microscope.

or (iii) the **object** of a **preposition**.

	OBJECT OF PREPOSITION	
She sat	*near* **me**	on the bus.
The letter was	*for* **us**	
I saw him give it	*to* **you**	last night.
It all depends	*on* **him**	
Paul went	*with* **her**	to the station.
They left	*without* **it**	
I have no complaints	*against* **them**	personally.

◉ *Looking at meaning*

Personal pronouns in the first and second person ('I'/'me', 'you', 'we'/'us') are often used in an interpersonal way to develop a relationship between speaker and listener, writer and reader (eg 'I am, **you** are, **we** are Australians'). In this extract, for example, we can see how the writer is trying to engage the reader by using personal pronouns:

> Of all the beautiful insects (we) see from time to time in gardens, in parks, or during our rambles in the countryside, none would appear to have the same attraction for (us) as do the butterflies and moths.
>
> Because these insects are so highly favoured (I) am giving them first place and dealing with them at length, but before (we) go on to the more practical side of the work (I) will discuss briefly the subject of English and scientific names and life-history, as this will enable (you) to have a better understanding of what is to follow …
>
> Let (me) tell you at once that (you) have absolutely no need whatever to be alarmed by scientific names. In fact (I) advise (you) to make use of them on all occasions, as by doing so they will soon be second nature to (you.)

C. V. A. Adams

In the following poems, notice how the personal pronouns 'I' and 'me' are being used in defining the writer's identity:

Spiritual Song of the Aborigine

I am a child of the Dreamtime People
Part of this land, like the gnarled gumtree
I am the river, softly singing
Chanting our songs on my way to the sea
My spirit is the dust-devils
Mirages, that dance on the plain
I'm the snow, the wind and the falling rain
I'm part of the rocks and the red desert earth
Red as the blood that flows in my veins
I am eagle, crow and snake that glides
Through the rainforest that clings to the
mountainside
There was emu, wombat, kangaroo
No other man of a different hue
I am this land
And this land is **me**
I am Australia.

Hyllus Maris

I am ...

I am all the things of my past –
the light hair of my dad.
I am all **I** see and hear –
my dog jumping and licking people
and running around the yard
going crazy;
Charlie and Olga arguing all the time,
police sirens wailing in the street,
cars conking out in the middle of the street,
I am all **I** have been taught and remember –
trying to speak proper Italian,
starting primary school,
and everyone crying.

Rosie Martorana

Personal pronouns (third person) can also be used to develop links within a text and make it cohesive. (See section about Cohesion on page 107.)

Possessive pronouns

 *Formation*

	SINGULAR	PLURAL
1st person *('speaking')*	mine	ours
2nd person *('spoken to')*	yours	yours
3rd person *('spoken of')*	his/hers	theirs

Looking at meaning

Possessive pronouns can replace a noun group to indicate ownership.

> That's not her purse, it's **mine** [my purse]!
> You've got your dinner, now we want **ours** [our dinner].
> My receipt has just arrived—when do you get **yours** [your receipt]?
> This is Michael's T-shirt. **Hers** [her T-shirt] is in the washing machine.

These are similar to the possessive determiners which we met earlier in the noun group (eg it's **my** purse), but in the case of possessive pronouns, they replace the noun group and are not followed by a noun (eg it's **mine**).

Relative pronouns

The main relative pronouns are **who, whom, whose, that**, and **which**. We have already met these in the section on adjectival clauses.

Who and **whom** refer to persons. **Who** is the subject and **whom** is the object.

> The person **who** was just speaking ... *(SUBJECT of VERB 'was speaking')*
> The person **whom** I drove to the station ... *(OBJECT of VERB 'drove')*
> The person to **whom** he gave the briefcase ... *(OBJECT of PREPOSITION 'to')*

These days it is common not to use the 'whom' form, particularly in spoken language (eg 'The person [who] I drove to the station'; 'The person [who] he gave the briefcase to').

That can be used with either people or things.

> The person **that** I want to meet ...
> The train **that** was late ...

Whose (the possessive form) can be used with people or things:

> People **whose** opinion I respect ...
> A country **whose** population is growing ...

Which is generally only used with things. Its form does not change whether it is subject or object.

> The flowers **which** were in that vase ... *(SUBJECT of VERB 'were')*
> That book **which** you lent me ... *(OBJECT of VERB 'lent')*
> The town to **which** I was travelling ... *(OBJECT of PREPOSITION 'to')*

Question pronouns

The pronouns **who, whom, whose, what** and **which** are used when we want to ask a certain type of question (often called a 'wh–' question):

> **Who** knows the answer?
> To **whom** did you send it?
> **Whose** umbrella is this?
> **What** can you see?
> **Which** do you prefer?

These are sometimes called **interrogative** pronouns.

Other pronouns

Other types of pronouns are not treated here in detail. Some students (eg ESL students), however, might experience difficulties with these pronouns.

- demonstrative pronouns
  (eg Do you want **these**? **That** is wrong. **Those** will do.)

- reflexive pronouns
  (eg myself, ourselves, yourself, yourselves, himself, herself, themselves)

- indefinite pronouns
  (eg anybody, anything, nobody, somebody, nothing, something, everybody, none)

- distributive pronouns
  (eg each, every, either, neither)

- reciprocal pronouns
  (eg each other, one another, the other)

- quantity pronouns
  (eg I'll have **three**, please. Give him **both**.)

Students should be supported to develop their understanding and use of pronouns within context rather than in sentence-level exercises.

Early primary

Learning to ...

Most students at this stage will be able to use quite confidently the full range of personal pronouns, though in the spoken language of some students there will be certain dialectal differences (eg 'yous', 'dem'). In their written texts students might not always use pronouns appropriately to refer back (eg 'Kangaroos are big. It has a strong tail.') They might be less confident with possessive, relative and interrogative/question pronouns, particularly if they are of non-English-speaking background.

Learning about ...

There is no need at this stage to explicitly discuss pronouns, though in shared and guided reading, students' attention could be drawn to how pronouns usually refer back to something previously mentioned in the text so that they are able to 'track' the participants. (See section about Cohesion on page 106.)

Mid primary

Learning to ...

Students should have no difficulties in competently using personal pronouns and most question and possessive pronouns by this stage but may still be coming to grips with certain types of relative pronouns (eg whose, whom, where). When reading, some students will 'skip over' the pronouns and start to lose the thread of the text. ESL students will often need help with pronouns (eg differentiating between masculine and feminine, between singular and plural, between subject and object).

Learning about ...

While it is not necessary for students to be familiar with the names of the different types of pronouns, it might be useful to explicitly model the full range so that they can become accustomed to their use. It might be of interest to point out the difference between subject pronouns and object pronouns, for example when explaining why sentences such as 'me and him went to the pictures' or 'She spoke to him and I' are not standard English.

Later primary

Learning to ...

By now students should be using most types of common pronouns competently, and should be attempting to use those pronouns listed in the section 'Other Pronouns'. Many ESL students will still need help with all types of pronouns.

Learning about ...

Students could be introduced to the names and functions of various types of pronouns at the teacher's discretion if this is perceived to be useful (eg the use of relative pronouns at the beginning of adjectival clauses—and how these can be sometimes omitted).

Verb groups

So far we have been looking at the different components of the noun group. Now we will move on to explore the verb group: the core of the clause.

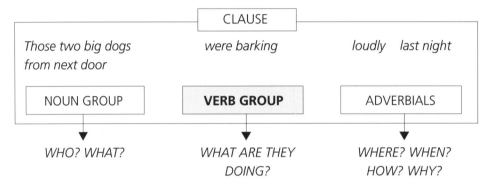

	CLAUSE	
Those two big dogs from next door	*were barking*	*loudly last night*
NOUN GROUP	**VERB GROUP**	ADVERBIALS
▼	▼	▼
WHO? WHAT?	*WHAT ARE THEY DOING?*	*WHERE? WHEN? HOW? WHY?*

A verb generally refers to an action or state. With younger children we can use the term 'doing word' (though this isn't always an accurate description).

A verb group can consist of a single word (eg He **wrote** a letter.) or a number of words (eg He **might have been going to talk**.).

Types of verbs

👁 *Looking at meaning*

When we are interested in how language functions to represent the world, we look at how different types of verbs are involved in expressing different aspects of our experience:

- action verbs
- saying verbs
- sensing verbs (eg thinking verbs, feeling verbs, perceiving verbs)
- relating verbs

In the following sections we look at each of these in turn.

👁 Action verbs

When we are talking about 'doings' and 'happenings' we use action verbs. These generally represent those more physical actions which we can observe around us. They are often found in the action sequence of a story:

> [The Seven young Parrots] began to fight, and they scuffled, and huffled, and ruffled, and shuffled, and puffled, and muffled, and buffled, and duffled, and fluffled, and guffled, and bruffled, and screamed, and shrieked, and squealed, and squeaked, and clawed, and snapped, and bit, and bumped, and thumped, and dumped, and flumped each other, till they were all torn into little bits.
>
> *Edward Lear*

The poem below provides an opportunity to extend the students' range of action verbs to bring the text to life and to help the reader to visualise what is going on.

Skateboard

We **twist**
   and we **turn**
      and the pavement
         we **burn**
            as we **rocket**
         downhill at a rate.
      We **whoop**
   and we **swoop**
as we **crouch**
and we **stoop**
   on the board
      where we **ride**
         when we **skate**.
With a shove
   and a run
      it is furious fun
         as we **roll**
            with a sweep
               and a swerve.
               Then we **reel**
               and we **rip**
            in a breathtaking trip
         while keeping
      our balance
      and nerve
   We **swing**
and we **sway**
in a dare-devil way
   on a hair-raising,
      zig-zagging track.
         Our father
         once **tried**.
         You'll find him
         inside
         with a very
         large bruise
         on his back.

               Max Fatchen

If we want to build up a character in a particular way, we might use more 'evaluative' action verbs where we express a judgement. For example, rather than saying 'Sam **walked** down the street', we can represent Sam positively ('Sam **skipped** down the street') or negatively ('Sam **slunk** down the street').

In recounts, action verbs predominate because recounts are generally about 'what happened':

> On Tuesday Kindergarten children and teachers **went** to Blue Gum Farm. We **fed** the cow. We **held** a chicken. We **patted** the horse.

Students might be encouraged to think carefully about which actions and happenings to include and which verbs might best express those actions.

Procedures are mainly about actions in the form of commands:

> **Put** the soil into the container.
> **Add** water to the soil.
> **Mix** the soil and water together.

Here the action verbs often need to be quite precise so that the procedure will be successful (eg 'dice' or 'slice' instead of simply 'cut').

In literary texts we often find action verbs being used in a metaphorical way:

> **Newtown — a Fantasy**
>
> Sunset
> **slides** over
> the slow stone
> cottages of Newtown.
> An aura of light
> **clings** to sloping
> chimney tops.
> Reluctant footsteps
> **linger**. Traffic
> noises *dim*. Open
> windows **catch** and
> **hold** the twilight.
> The sun **tangles**
> in a Port Jackson
> fig tree a few
> houses down. All
> the colours of the rainbow
> **run** berserk over the
> slow stone cottages
> of Newtown.
>
> *Colleen Burke*

> **The Sea**
>
> Deep glass-green seas
> **chew** rocks
> with their green-glass jaws.
> But little waves
> **creep** in
> and **nibble** softly at the sand.
>
> *Lilith Norman*

The following are some common action verbs:

take	get	run	come	make
live	work	do	shake	fly
slip	give	eat	drive	blow
look	rub	buy	read	play

Saying verbs

Sometimes experience is not represented directly, but is reported through someone else's words. Saying verbs are found most commonly in stories, where we get to know the characters by the way they speak. In the following passage, for example, Lewis Carroll could have simply said that Alice was a polite girl who was eager to please and the Mouse was an impatient, thin-skinned creature, but instead he gives us insights into their personalities and their relationship through the way they talk to and about each other:

> "You are not attending!" **said** the Mouse to Alice severely. "What are you thinking of?"
> "I beg your pardon," **said** Alice very humbly: "you had got to the fifth bend, I think?"
> "I had not!" **cried** the Mouse, angrily.
> "A knot!" **said** Alice, always trying to make herself useful, and looking anxiously about her. "Oh, do let me help to undo it!"
> "I shall do nothing of the sort," **said** the Mouse, getting up and walking away. "You insult me by talking such nonsense!"
> "I didn't mean it!" **pleaded** poor Alice. "But you're so easily offended, you know!"
> The Mouse only growled in reply.
> "Please come back and finish your story!" Alice **called** after it.
>
> *Lewis Carroll*

In guided reading, you could point out the different saying verbs used (eg pleaded, whispered, responded, sighed) and discuss how these can be more effective than 'said'. You could also look at the adverbials used with saying verbs which help to build up the character and mood (eg severely, humbly, angrily, in a languid, sleepy voice, rather eagerly, in a soothing tone). Wordbanks could be assembled for the students to use later in their own writing.

Saying verbs are also important in newspaper articles, where it is reported what people said (or promised, or threatened, or implied, or announced). This could become part of a media study unit (eg involving a critical evaluation of how people's 'sayings' are reported).

When looking at saying verbs, we can also deal with such matters as the difference between direct and indirect speech, and the punctuation of direct speech. (See section on Quoting and Reporting, page 97.)

The following are some common saying verbs:

say	cry	scream	shout	whisper
plead	stammer	explain	suggest	imply
report	murmur	ask	tell	promise
claim	deny	respond	reply	continue

👁 Sensing verbs

Sensing verbs are used only in relation to humans, describing their thoughts, opinions, beliefs, feelings, and so on. They can feature in arguments and discussions (eg It is thought that ...; I believe that ...) where we are interested in people's ideas. They are not commonly found in information reports and other more factually oriented texts.

Sensing verbs can give us insight into the characters of a story by describing what is going on in their minds. They are often used when characters reflect on the action or evaluate what is happening in the story.

> "I **wish** the monstrous crow would come!" **thought** Alice.
> "There's only one sword, you **know**," said Tweedledum to his brother: "but you can have the umbrella — it's quite as sharp. Only we must begin quick. It's getting as dark as it can."
> It was getting dark so suddenly that Alice **thought** there must be a thunderstorm coming on. "What a thick black cloud that is!" she said. "And how fast it comes! Why, I **do believe** it's got wings!" ... Alice ran a little way into the wood, and stopped under a large tree. "It can never get me here," she **thought**. "But I **wish** it wouldn't flap its wings so."
>
> ......
>
> By this time it was getting light. "The crow must have flown away, I **think**," said Alice: "I'm so glad it's gone. I **thought** it was the night coming on."
>
> "I **wish** I could manage to be that glad!" the Queen said. "Only I never **can remember** the rule. You must be very happy, living in this wood, and being glad whenever you **like**!"
>
> *Lewis Carroll*

We are not only interested in people's thoughts but in their feelings—particularly in literary texts.

> I **hate** to scrub the dishes
> I **hate** to scrub the floor
> But I **love** to kiss my boyfriend
> Behind the kitchen door door door.
> *All Right, Vegemite!*

We could also include verbs of perception—those which involve the use of our five senses: seeing, hearing, tasting, feeling, smelling.

The following are some common sensing verbs:

think	believe	wish	remember	wonder
know	forget	see	consider	perceive
reflect	imagine	recollect	recall	understand
comprehend	decide	realise	hypothesise	assume
feel	want	like	frighten	enjoy
love	hate	fear	despise	loathe
hurt	please	upset	amuse	disgust
hear	taste	smell	see	observe

Relating verbs

There are some verbs which do not represent actions, speaking, thoughts or feelings. Their job is to simply link two pieces of information. We can call these 'relating verbs'. (In other grammars, they are referred to as relational processes or link verbs.)

The most common relating verbs are the verbs 'to be' and 'to have'. These are frequently found in information reports and descriptions, where the emphasis is on providing information about something.

The relating verb might link two noun groups:

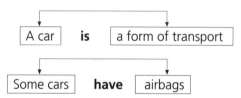

Or it might link a noun group to an adjectival:

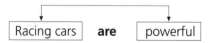

Sometimes a relating verb relates a noun group to an adverbial (eg of place):

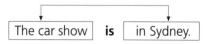

This type of clause is critical in school learning as it is a major resource for defining, describing, classifying, exemplifying and summarising. It is the major clause type found in information reports.

Sometimes the relationship between two things is expressed by other verbs:

The girls **became** good friends.
Four leaf clovers **represent** good luck.
The colour red **symbolises** the land.
The sky **grew** darker.
Eagles **possess** strong beaks.
She **seems** happy enough.
The bread **tastes** stale.
The flowers **smelled** heavenly.
I **felt** sore all over.
It **sounds** fishy to me.
She **is called** Bunny.

The following are some common relating verbs:

be	have	possess	include	represent
mean	look	symbolises	become	results in
turn into	equal	seem	appear	remain
taste	feel	smell	sound	call

Note: A related type of verb is where there is no action or relationship being described, simply a state:

There is a hole in your jeans.
There are no decent shows on television.
There was nothing to do.

These are typically introduced by 'there' and are sometimes called 'existing' verbs (or existentials).

Having looked at different types of verbs and the meanings they construct, let's now explore the information contained in the verb group.

Tense

Tense tells us about time—when an action takes place. The verb group tells us whether something is happening in the **present**, the **past**, or the **future**.

With younger students it will be sufficient to be able to refer generally to these three tenses. With older students, however, it might be necessary to distinguish between different types of present, past and future tenses. It is not necessary that every student be taught systematically about all the aspects of tenses included here. It is, however, knowledge which you as a teacher will need when identifying the nature of problems which certain students might be having with their use of verbs. You may want to be able to explain how a particular tense is formed in English or how it is used in different ways. Or you may want to extend students' ability to use a wider range of tenses to lend precision and interest to their writing. In these cases, you will need to decide how much your students need to know about the types, formation and use of tenses.

 Formation

Present

Most English verbs have two present tenses: the **present simple** (or simple present) and the **present continuous** (or present progressive).

Present simple

The present simple is generally formed using a single word:

> I **read** the papers every day.
> Fish **have** gills.
> They **like** the footy.
> Belinda **is** absent today.
> She **has** a cold.

Most verbs in the present simple are fairly regular. The verb 'to be', however, is irregular:

	SINGULAR		PLURAL	
1st person	*I*	am	*we*	are
2nd person	*you*	are	*you*	are
3rd person	*he/she/it*	is	*they*	are

Present continuous

The present continuous is formed by using a helping verb (the auxiliary verb 'to be') and a present participle (ending in –*ing*):

	HELPING VERB (AUXILIARY)	PRESENT PARTICIPLE
he	is	going
they	are	finishing
we	are	hoping
I	am	doing
she	is	having
you	are	taking

Note: It is important not to confuse the verb 'to be' used as a helping verb ('I **am** coming') with the verb 'to be' used as a relating verb (eg 'I **am** angry'—see p.58).

Past

There are several past tenses in English. Here we will focus only on the three most common—**past simple**, **past continuous**, and **perfect**—though students need to recognise that other past tenses exist. Most students of English-speaking background will not have any problems forming the past tense—particularly of regular verbs. Some students might need assistance, however, with irregular verbs and with when to use the different types of past tense.

Past simple

The past simple is generally formed by adding –**ed** to the stem of the verb:

STEM OF VERB		PAST SIMPLE
walk	➤	walk**ed**
visit	➤	visit**ed**
work	➤	work**ed**

If the verb stem ends in –**e**, simply add **d**:

use	➤	use**d**
decide	➤	decide**d**

If the verb ends in a **stressed vowel + consonant**, double the consonant and add –**ed**:

plan	➤	pla**nned**
prefer	➤	prefe**rred**

If the verb ends in a **consonant + –y**, change the y to an i and add –**ed**:

study	➤	stud**ied**
try	➤	tr**ied**

Troubleshooting

A major problem for some students is the fact that there are many irregular verbs in the past simple tense, eg:

be	→	was/were	know	→	knew
begin	→	began	learn	→	learnt/learned
break	→	broke	lend	→	lent
bring	→	brought	make	→	made
buy	→	bought	put	→	put
catch	→	caught	read	→	read
come	→	came	run	→	ran
dig	→	dug	say	→	said
do	→	did	see	→	saw
eat	→	ate	speak	→	spoke
feel	→	felt	stand	→	stood
find	→	found	swim	→	swam
get	→	got	teach	→	taught
have	→	had	wear	→	wore

Past continuous

The past continuous tense is formed by using the past tense of a helping verb (the auxiliary verb 'to be'—**was/were**) plus the present participle:

He **was reading** that book all night.
We **were hoping** you would come.

	HELPING VERB (AUXILIARY)	PRESENT PARTICIPLE
he	was	going
they	were	finishing
we	were	hoping
I	was	doing
she	was	having
you	were	taking

Perfect tense

The perfect tense is formed by using the helping verb 'to have' plus the past participle:

We **have visited** Rome before.
I **have done** the dishes.

	HELPING VERB (AUXILIARY)	PRESENT PARTICIPLE
he	has	gone
they	have	finished
we	have	promised
I	have	felt
she	has	had
you	have	been

Other past tenses

There are other variations on the above tenses which are used to express subtle differences about when an action took place, eg:

- *perfect continuous*
  I **have been waiting** now for an hour.

- *past perfect*
  I **had told** him that I would wait.

- *past perfect continuous*
  I **had been waiting** for two hours when he finally arrived.

For habitual actions in the past, the forms 'used to + verb' or 'would + verb' can be used, as in this excerpt from *The Whalers* which describes how the killer whales used to help the Aboriginal whalers:

> The dark people **would never go lookin'** for whales. The killers **would let them know** if there were whales about. Ole Uncle **would speak** to them killers in the language. They must have been *bugeens*, clever blackfellers. They**'d go** as far as Narooma lookin' for whales. Two **would stop** with the whale and one **would go back** to Twofold Bay an' **leap out of** the water. 'Pook-urr!' He**'d slap** his tail an' let the whalers know.
>
> *Rowland Robinson*

It is unlikely that primary students will need to be able to name or discuss these different past tenses, but it is expected that they should be able to interpret and use them appropriately within the context of reading and writing relevant texts.

Future

The future tense is formed by using the helping verb 'will' plus the main verb:

She **will be** on holidays in December.
I**'ll do** it when I'm ready!

	HELPING VERB (AUXILIARY)	**MAIN VERB**
he	will	go
they	will	finish
we	will	promise
I	will	read
she	will	have
you	will	be

In some English dialects, the auxiliary 'shall' is used with the first person ('I **shall** read'; 'we **shall** promise'), though in present-day Australia it is no longer insisted upon.

There are other ways of referring to the future in English. We can also use the present continuous tense ('I **am seeing** James on Thursday'), the present simple tense ('We **leave** at six tomorrow'), the verb 'going' ('I **am going to see** James on Thursday'), or 'be about' for events in the very near future ('I**'m about to leave**'). This can be a confusing area for ESL students.

Look at how the following poem uses three different verb forms to refer to future time:

When I **grow up**
I**'m going to be** rich and famous
By inventing the antidote
To the common chocolate.

But until then
I**'ll eat** as many as I can
And call it
Research.

Bill Condon

Modals

Modals give us information about the degree of obligation or certainty involved in the action. If we feel a bit tentative about doing something, we can use low modality, eg:

> I **might** go.
> He **could** be angry.
> You **may** want to look into it.

If we want to express a high degree of certainty, we can use high modality, eg:

> I **must** go.
> He **will** be angry.
> You **ought** to look into it.

 *Formation*

Modals are formed by using a modal auxiliary plus the verb.

Here is a list of some modal auxiliaries:

HIGH MODALITY	MEDIUM MODALITY	LOW MODALITY
must	will	may
ought to	should	might
shall	can	could
has to	need to	would

Modality can also be expressed through other grammatical resources:

- *modal **nouns***
  eg possibility, probability, obligation, necessity, requirement

- *modal **adjectives***
  eg possible, probable, obligatory, necessary, required, determined

- *modal **adverbs***
  eg possibly, probably, perhaps, maybe, sometimes, always, never, certainly, definitely

Looking at meaning

In any particular situation, we choose different degrees of modality depending on how we want to relate to the listener/reader and how we want to portray our own level of commitment to an idea or action. Someone with a high degree of authority, status, power or expertise may choose to use high modality in order to convince someone to do something or to believe something. In other situations, low modality might leave open the possibility of negotiation.

Knowing how to use modality appropriately is something which students take a long time to master as it involves making judgements about personal relationships and how to interact with others in appropriate ways. It is an interesting aspect of language to explore when examining a text critically—who uses high modality? who uses low modality? why? with what effect?

It is important to be able to choose the appropriate degree of modality in text types which involve persuading people and making judgements, such as discussions, expositions, advertisements and narratives.

Negative forms

As well as using verbs in the positive form, we can make them negative.

 Formation

When we form the negative, we generally insert the word 'not' after the helping (auxiliary) verb, eg:

> I **will not listen** any longer.
> They **have not remembered** their books.
> We **were not doing** anything.

With those tenses which do not use a helping verb, however, we also need to insert the verb 'do/does' when forming the negative:

- *present simple*

  > I **play** the piano. → I **do not play** the piano.
  > He **likes** bananas. → He **does not like** bananas.

- *past simple*

  > She **worked** hard. → She **did not work** hard.
  > They **came** home. → They **did not come** home.

Negatives, of course, can be contracted:

> They **have not remembered**. → They **haven't remembered**.
> We **were not doing** anything. → We **weren't doing** anything.
> I **do not play** the piano. → I **don't play** the piano.
> He **does not like** bananas. → He **doesn't like** bananas.
> She **did not work** hard. → She **didn't work** hard.
> They **did not come** home. → They **didn't come** home.

The contraction of the negative in the future tense is irregular:

> She **will not eat** her dinner. → She **won't eat** her dinner.

Some students (particularly those of non-English-speaking background) might need to be taught the rules of contraction and when to use contractions (eg in spoken language and more informal written texts).

In some cases it might be necessary to point out that, particularly in written texts, we don't use a double negative in Standard Australian English:

'I did**n't** say **nothing**.'

 Looking at meaning

In terms of meaning, the negative often has the function of introducing an interpersonal tone involving contradiction, disapproval, opposition, denial, absence, and so on, where the speaker/writer is making a judgement about the truth or value of a statement. This negative tenor is often found in text-types such as discussions and expositions:

Birds should **not** be kept in cages.
One should **never** forget …

Other negative words include:

neither	nor	no	nobody	nowhere
never	none	not	no one	nothing

Prefixes and suffixes can also contribute a negative tone:

We were very **dis**pleased.
That was **un**fortunate.
It's a worth**less** piece of rubbish.

Multiword verbs

Sometimes a verb group is made up of several words. As we have seen, this can be due to the need to indicate tense (eg 'has gone', 'will be looking'). But sometimes it simply takes more than one word to express the meaning of the verb (eg 'tried to move', 'stood up'). This is not a major grammatical point to be taught, but it does help when trying to identify where the verb group begins and ends—ie the boundaries of the verb group.

 Formation

Complex verbs

Some verb groups consist of two verbs, each of which contributes to the meaning, eg:

The babies **began crying** when they heard the thunder.
He **started to sing**, but his voice faltered.
They **had finished eating**.
She **tried to warn** them.
We **aim to please**.
It **seems to be** correct.

As you can see, the verb group can become quite lengthy:

He **has been wanting to get started** all morning.
Maggie **might have been trying to say** something important.

Verbs with adverbs or prepositions

Sometimes a verb group will consist of a verb plus an adverb or a preposition, eg:

She **woke** *up* at nine.
They finally **backed** *down*.
I **rang** *up* Di but she **had gone** *out*.
Put the dishes *away*.
Take *down* the washing.
The gangsters **handed** *over* the money.
He **cut** *down* the tree.
He **was fighting** *off* the flu.
The cat **knocked** *over* the milk.

Technically, these are called phrasal verbs and can cause problems for some ESL students. They are very common in spoken language and can make a written text sound somewhat informal. Students could be introduced to more formal alternatives eg ring up/telephone; put off/delay; bring down/decrease; knock down/defeat; run away/disappear; come in/enter; plug in/insert.

'Empty' verb plus noun

Some verbs are formed by using 'empty' verbs such as 'have' or 'do' with a noun, eg:

Have a look at this!
She **is having a shower** now.
They **did a dance** and then **took a bow**.
She **made a vow** that she **would keep her promise**.
He **gave a loud laugh**.
I **gave a nod** and **took my leave**.

In this case the main meaning of the action is actually expressed through the noun. These are also more common in spoken language and often have more formal alternatives:

I gave a nod   ➤   I **nodded**.

Summary: Verb groups in a text

Text 1: Narrative

relating verb

It [was] a lovely pool, in a large, glassed-in room

with windows facing a garden. There [were] floating toys — *existing verb*

and big plastic balls in the water. She [cleared] them to one side — *action verb*

sensing verb (feeling)

and [enjoyed] the luxury of [having] a whole indoor pool to herself. *relating verb (possessive)*

action verb

She [swam about] grandly, [pretending] she [was] Megan.

action verb

Megan's mother [had never had to go out to work] in her life. *sensing verb (thinking)*

relating verb (possessive) Megan [had] everything.

relating verb

Half an hour later she [became] aware of a tapping on the centre — *relating verb*

relating verb

window. Ben [was] out in the garden, [peering] worriedly at her, — *action verb*

relating verb

his face against the glass. She [ignored] him, but he [didn't go away,] — *action verb*

action verb

and the tapping [became] louder. She [scowled,] [got out of] the pool — *sensing verb*

action verb

and [opened] the window. — *action verb*

action verb

"Listen, you!" she [said.] "I [won't drown] in this dumb pool!

relating verb

The water['s] hardly over my head, even down the deep end. — *saying verb*

Now [nick off!"]

action verb

Robin Klein

Text 2: Information report

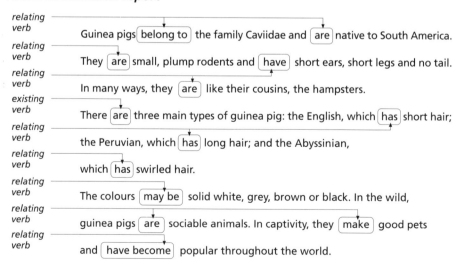

relating verb

Guinea pigs [belong to] the family Caviidae and [are] native to South America.

relating verb

They [are] small, plump rodents and [have] short ears, short legs and no tail.

relating verb

In many ways, they [are] like their cousins, the hampsters.

existing verb

There [are] three main types of guinea pig: the English, which [has] short hair;

relating verb

the Peruvian, which [has] long hair; and the Abyssinian,

relating verb

which [has] swirled hair.

relating verb

The colours [may be] solid white, grey, brown or black. In the wild,

relating verb

guinea pigs [are] sociable animals. In captivity, they [make] good pets

relating verb

and [have become] popular throughout the world.

Early Primary

Learning to ...

Most students should be using an increasing range of verbs to represent common activities. Students should demonstrate the ability to express finer distinctions (eg 'wriggle', 'slither', 'twist' or 'turn' instead of simply 'move'). Their writing may contain simple verb groups using tenses appropriate to a particular text type.

Learning about ...

In their writing, reading and viewing, they should be able to recognise words and visuals which express an action. In these discussions, terms such as 'doing words' could be used, though they could gradually be introduced to the term 'verb' or 'verb group'. Students could be encouraged to talk about simple verbs of various types where appropriate (eg action verbs, saying verbs, thinking verbs).

Mid Primary

Learning to ...

Most students should be comprehending and employing a wide variety of verbs in both oral and written modes. They will be using a number of different tenses quite appropriately, but the range of possibilities might need to be modelled. Their use of modality might be quite basic at this point.

Learning about ...

By now, students should be learning to name the different types of verbs encountered and to understand how verb groups are structured. Students should be able to differentiate between action verbs, saying verbs, and sensing (thinking/ feeling/ perceiving) verbs and to discuss the different meanings that these contribute to the text. They should recognise relating verbs and understand how these are used to link one piece of information to another (eg in descriptions, definitions, classifications, and so on). They might speculate about which types of verbs can be found in which type of text and why. They should know how to spell the third person singular of verbs and the negative form (including contractions). They should be able to recognise how verbs can be formed by using prefixes and suffixes.

Later Primary

Learning to ...

Most students should be understanding and employing a wide repertoire of different types of verbs. They should be able to select those verbs which are most appropriate to express fine distinctions and detail (eg 'grumbled', 'growled' or 'thundered' instead of 'said'). In factual texts they should be comprehending and using more technical verbs (eg 'expand', 'contract', 'repel', 'magnetise'). In literary texts they should be appreciating and attempting to use verbs which best develop the character, mood, action sequences, image, and so on. They should be comprehending and constructing detailed verb groups which include more sophisticated use of tense and modality. They should be familiar with the past simple tense and past participles of most common irregular verbs. If their writing sounds 'childish' because of overuse of phrasal verbs and 'empty' verbs, they could be introduced to more formal alternatives.

Learning about ...

Students should be able to reflect on and discuss the selection of different types of verbs in texts they are reading and writing and how they can function to develop a topic, to influence the listener/reader, to add precision, and so on. They should be able to identify verbs which are technical. They should be able to recognise the function of different parts of the verb group, including a range of auxiliary verbs and modals. Some students might benefit from knowing about complex verb groups and phrasal verbs. They should be familiar with a number of common Latin and Greek roots.

Adverbials

Adverbials are those words and phrases provide extra detail about what is going on ('where?', 'when?', 'how?', 'why?', 'with whom?', 'by what means?', 'for how long?', and so on.).

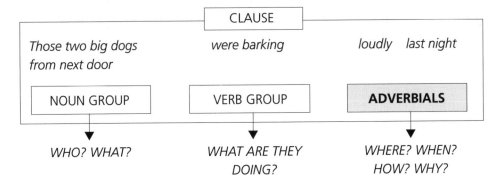

Types of adverbials

There are two main categories of adverbials:

- adverbs
- adverbial phrases

Adverbs

Formation

Adverbs generally consist of a single word:

tomorrow	upstairs	quickly	there
soon	probably	well	finally

Adverbs are often formed by adding **–ly** to the end of an adjective:

stupid → stupidly
thankful → thankfully

Note that when the adjective ends in **–y**, you need to change the 'y' to 'i' before adding 'ly':

happy → happily
angry → angrily

Adverbial phrases

🔲 Formation

Adverbial phrases are expressed by a group of words generally beginning with a preposition:

near the house
at five o'clock
in a deep voice
with her mother

Prepositions are generally single words (eg on, in, under) but can sometimes be multiple words (eg on top of, in front of). The following is a list of common prepositions:

at	of	to	by	with
from	about	in	beside	for
into	until	near	under	during
like	on	after	above	across
along	among	around	before	behind
below	beneath	between	down	inside
off	past	through	towards	up
within	away from	close by	in front of	on top of
all over	close to	near to	out of	next to

You may have noticed that both adjectival phrases and adverbial phrases are typically expressed by a **preposition** plus a **noun group** (ie a prepositional phrase). They do different jobs however. An adjectival phrase describes a noun (eg 'He was talking to <u>the girl</u> **from New York**') while an adverbial phrase provides information about the verb (eg 'She <u>came</u> **from New York**').

Adverbial roles

Adverbials can play a number of different roles in a clause.

Modifying the verb

The main function of adverbials is to tell us more about the verb (or more technically, they **modify** verbs).

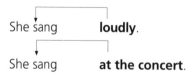

She sang   **loudly**.

She sang   **at the concert**.

Apart from adding meaning to verbs, adverbials can take on various other roles in the clause such as modifying an adjective, modifying another adverb, and modifying the sentence as a whole.

Modifying an adjective

Adverbs can modify adjectives:

> She was **too** *clever* for words.
> His face was **very** *red*.
> I was **a little** *scared*.
> They were **terribly** *tired*.
> Margaret was **more** *sympathetic*.

Modifying another adverb

Adverbs can also modify other adverbs.

> The family **almost** *always* had porridge for breakfast.
> He spoke **very** *highly* of you.
> We ate *well* **enough**.
> He was running **too** *slowly*.
> They worked **awfully** *hard*.
> She talks **very much more** *openly* these days.

Both the above groups of adverbs belong to the 'degree' type—see page 77.

Modifying a sentence

Sometimes adverbials function to set the tone for the whole sentence. They often signal to the listener or reader how to interpret a statement.

> **From my point of view**, he's wrong.
> **Technically**, it was a fault.
> **Politically** it was a smart move.
> **According to her**, they were all quite satisfied.
> **In my opinion**, we should just forget about it.
> **Frankly** I think he's a bore.
> **In a strange way**, I really respect him.

Functions of adverbials

👁 *Looking at meaning*

In terms of meaning, one of the major functions of adverbs and adverbial phrases is to provide information about the circumstances surrounding an action, eg:

- place (where?)
- time (when? how long? how often?)
- manner (how? by what means? like what?)
- cause (why?)
- accompaniment (with whom?)

Some examples are given over the page.

ADVERBIALS		
	ADVERB	**ADVERBIAL PHRASE**
Place		
WHERE?	here indoors there upstairs backwards inside out forwards nearby away inside	over there into the garden at home out of the window under the chair
Time		
WHERE?	soon yesterday tomorrow afterwards today later already suddenly now early then beforehand	in the evening at ten o'clock by midnight on Tuesday about midday before dinner
HOW LONG?	forever no longer still any longer yet any more already so far overnight briefly	for a week since last Friday the whole day/all day until yesterday during/throughout the war
HOW OFTEN?	frequently a lot twice increasingly daily hardly ever never much always occasionally sometimes rarely often seldom usually	every day on Sundays from time to time at weekends in the evenings day by day
Manner		
IN WHAT WAY? (including qualities and feelings)	sadly swiftly quietly violently fast politely hard gently angrily reluctantly	with a sigh in a strange way without trying
BY WHAT MEANS?	thereby	with a broom by car
LIKE WHAT?	similarly differently	by way of contrast in comparison like a dream
Cause		
WHY?	thus therefore consequently accordingly hence	for that reason because of bad weather from old age/of old age through mismanagement as a result of his pleading due to her efforts
Accompaniment		
WITH WHOM?	alone together	by himself with her mother

Other functions of adverbials

👁 *Looking at meaning*

Apart from providing information about the circumstances surrounding an action, adverbials perform other functions of a more interpersonal nature, such as indicating the speaker's attitude, adding emphasis, toning down a statement, limiting the scope, and so on.

👁 Viewpoint and comment adverbials

Some sentence adverbials express viewpoint and the speaker's attitude towards the topic, eg:

In my opinion, you're making a mistake.
Personally I think it's foolish.
Surprisingly he got away with it.
Hopefully we won't have to pay.

Other examples are:–

curiously	happily	hopefully	seriously	unfortunately
apparently	ideally	plainly	luckily	preferably
surely	in fairness	presumably	naturally	strangely
fortunately	ideally	no doubt	alas	surprisingly
admittedly	anyway	at least	ironically	naturally
oddly	of course	logically	unbelievably	significantly

These generally come at the beginning of the sentence, but not necessarily.

Adverbials of manner can also be used to express an opinion. Just as there are 'factual' and 'opinion' adjectives, so there are 'factual' and 'opinion' adverbials:

She cried **loudly**. (*factual*)
She cried **plaintively**. (*opinion*)

Adverbials of viewpoint, comment and opinion are important when considering how the speaker or writer can use language to influence the listener or reader.

👁 Degree adverbials

These are used to place more or less emphasis on a statement, eg:

I **completely** forgot to phone her.
They **almost** got away with it.

Some other examples are:

terribly	just	really	awfully	somewhat
deeply	dreadfully	half	incredibly	moderately
certainly	so	surely	obviously	plainly
nearly	quite	scarcely	practically	sort of
utterly	wonderfully	truly	reasonably	drastically
partly	perfectly	poorly	slightly	soundly
kind of	more or less	hardly	very	extremely
absolutely	rather	fairly	virtually	entirely
generally	typically	by and large	basically	overall
much	more	less	(the) most	(the) least
better	(the) best	worse	(the) worst	more or less

Sometimes these are used to distance the speaker and decrease commitment to the statement:

She was **somewhat** perplexed.
In a way, I was relieved that she left.
They were ratbags **so to speak**.
Up to a point I enjoy ballet.

Focusing and emphasising adverbials

These adverbials are used to focus attention on a certain aspect of the statement or to emphasise the importance of something, eg:

She **even** held his hand.
They're **only** going for a week.
He **just** wanted to say sorry.
I **simply** walked out of the room.
He **really** likes you.
I **especially** wanted to see the zebras.
Above all, don't believe everything he says.
She is not sick **at all**.
I am **mainly** interested in what you want to do.
They came **specially** to talk with you.

Modal adverbs

These indicate the degree of probability or obligation attached to a statement, eg:

probably	possibly	certainly	definitely	doubtless
maybe	no doubt	perhaps	presumably	really
allegedly	apparently	seemingly	undoubtedly	in fact
surely	positively	always	sometimes	never

(See page 66 on Modals.)

Summary: Adverbials in a text

In a narrative you would expect to find a range of adverbials doing a number of different jobs: providing information about the place and time that actions take place; indicating the manner in which actions are done; introducing the writer's perspective through comments and emphasis; tempering statements in terms of the degree of certainty; and so on. The following text uses adverbials both to build up a picture of 'reality' and to intrude the writer's viewpoint.

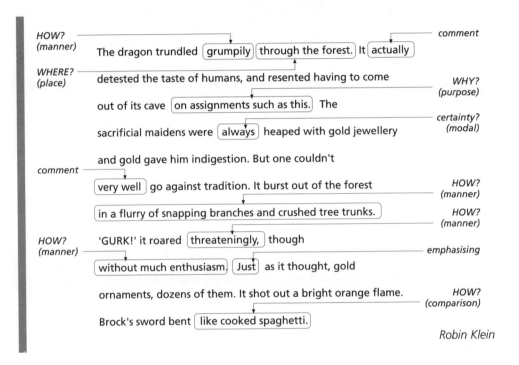

Robin Klein

Note: Some adverbials have not been analysed, such as those belonging to phrasal verbs ('to come out of', 'go against', 'burst out of', 'shot out').

Early Primary

Learning to ...

In their oral language, students will be using a wide variety of adverbials, both to describe actions and to express their personal perspective. Their writing may initially contain simple adverbials, for example, of place and time. But over time students should be able to use an increasing range of adverbials to describe common activities, (when? where? how?). Students should demonstrate the ability to express finer distinctions (eg 'swiftly', 'speedily', 'hastily' instead of simply 'quickly').

Learning about ...

In their writing, reading and viewing, students should be able to recognise words and visuals which describe when, where and how an action is done. In these discussions, terms such as 'when words', 'where words', 'how words' could be introduced, eventually introducing a term such as 'verb describer'.

Mid Primary

Learning to ...

Most students should be comprehending and employing a wide variety of adverbials in both oral and written modes. They will be using adverbials of place, time, manner, cause and accompaniment. They will be using simple forms of degree adverbs and focusing/emphasising adverbs. Their use of modality might be relatively basic at this stage.

Learning about ...

Students should be able to differentiate between simple adverbials and adjectivals. They should be able to identify the different functions of adverbials (eg providing information about an action in terms of where, when, how, why and with whom) and to discuss the way in which these contribute different meanings to the text. They should recognise simple degree adverbs (eg 'very', 'really', 'a little bit', 'slightly') and understand how these are used to indicate the strength of the statement. They might speculate about which types of adverbials can be found in which type of text and why (eg very precise and detailed adverbials in procedures, adverbs of manner when building up a character in a story). They should know that many adverbs are formed by adding –ly to an adjective and that adverbial phrases consist of a preposition plus a noun group. They might investigate different types of prepositions in adverbial phrases and make sure they are using them accurately. By now, students could be using more technical terms such as 'adverb' and 'adverbial phrase' (or even the more general term 'adverbial').

Later Primary

Learning to ...

Most students should be understanding and employing a wide repertoire of different types of adverbials. They should be able to select those adverbials which are most appropriate to express fine distinctions and detail (eg 'occasionally', 'from time to time', or 'hardly ever' instead of simply 'sometimes'). In factual texts they should be comprehending and using more precise adverbials (eg 'in the winter of 1965', 'due to global warming', 'for five minutes'). In literary texts they should be appreciating and attempting to use adverbials which best develop the character, mood, action sequences, image, and so on (eg 'she murmured **lazily**', '**in the icy depths of winter**'). Particularly in prepared oral presentation, they should be comprehending and constructing clauses which include more sophisticated use of adverbials (eg sentence adverbials which express the writer's perspective, comment adverbs, 'point of view' adverbs, degree adverbs, and modal adverbs).

Learning about ...

Students should be able to reflect on and discuss the selection of different types of adverbials in texts they are reading and writing and how they can function to tell us more about an experience (eg when? where? how? why? with whom?) or to influence the listener/reader (eg when the writer's attitude intrudes (comment adverbs) or when the writer emphasises or tones down a particular aspect of a statement (degree adverbs, focusing and emphasising adverbs), or when a writer uses high or low modality). They might not be expected to name these more 'interpersonal' types of adverbials, but they should be encouraged to explore the impact they have on a text. They should be able to arrange certain types of adverbials in a continuum (eg always, often, sometimes, seldom, hardly ever, never). Some students might benefit from knowing that adverbs can modify other categories (eg adjectives, other adverbs and whole sentences) as well as verbs.

Organising clauses

We have looked at the main components of the clause, but we haven't examined how these chunks fit together. We can approach this in two ways. Firstly in terms of the **syntax**—or how the clause is structured. And secondly, in terms of the **meaning**—or what choices are possible in creating different types of messages.

 *Formation*

Syntax

When we talk about syntax, we are mainly interested in how clauses are structured so that we can identify problems that students might have. A well-structured sentence, for example, must (generally) contain a **verb**. The verb will probably have a **subject**, ie a noun group or pronoun which comes before the verb:

Sasha	was reading.
SUBJECT	VERB

Sometimes there is also a noun following the verb. This is called the **object** of the verb:

Sasha	was reading	the newspaper.
SUBJECT	VERB	OBJECT

With certain verbs, it is possible to have two objects: a **direct object** and an **indirect object**:

Sasha	was reading	the newspaper	to Tim.
SUBJECT	VERB	DIRECT OBJECT	INDIRECT OBJECT

Sasha	was reading	Tim	the newspaper.
SUBJECT	VERB	INDIRECT OBJECT	DIRECT OBJECT

> My boyfriend gave me an apple,
> My boyfriend gave me a pear,
> My boyfriend gave me a kiss on the lips
> And threw me down the stairs.
>
> *All Right, Vegemite!*

Shifting emphasis by using the passive

In English, we have a choice between the active ('Police have warned residents ...') and the passive ('Residents have been warned by the police ...'):

ACTIVE: Police   **have warned**   residents ...

PASSIVE: Residents   **have been warned**   by police ...

While the meaning is much the same, the emphasis has shifted in the passive from the police to the residents. The passive is an important resource for shifting emphasis. It might be that we want to maintain the focus on a particular participant. It might be that the 'do-er' is not important and the emphasis should be on the 'done-to'.

The passive is found in texts such as newspaper stories, bureaucratic memos, historical accounts, and explanations (where the emphasis is not so much 'who is responsible' but rather 'what is the effect').

👁 *Looking at meaning*

We can also look at how the clause is organised in terms of meaning, and ask:

- how does a clause represent a particular slice of experience?
- what type of action is occurring?
- who is initiating the action?
- who is on the receiving end?
- who is saying what to whom?
- who is doing the thinking, feeling and perceiving?
- what are they thinking about?
- what are they feeling?
- what are they perceiving?
- what is being described, or defined, or classified?
- how?

These are questions often asked when looking at a text from a critical literacy perspective.

When students are learning to read, it is helpful if they can see the sentences in terms of meaningful chunks. It is not necessary that they use the terminology below, but that they are able to recognise how a clause is made up of units of meaning. This can be encouraged indirectly (eg pausing and intonation when the teacher is reading aloud) or more explicitly (eg asking students questions such as those above).

If we go back to the different verb types, we can see that each type involves different kinds of participants.

Clauses with action verbs

With an action verb, we could ask two questions

- 'who is doing the action?' ('**do-er**')
- 'who is receiving the action?' ('**done-to**')

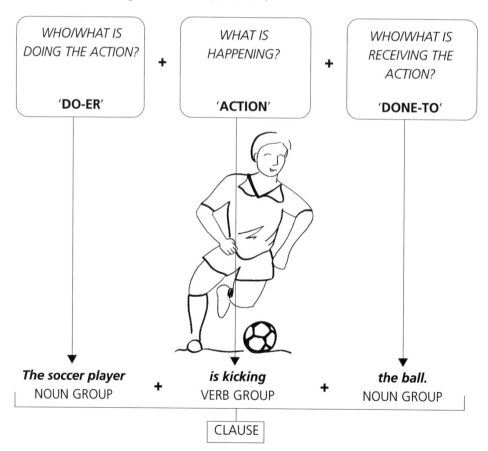

👁 Clauses with saying verbs

When we use saying verbs, we need to see that this type of verb represents a different kind of experience and involves different kinds of participants (ie the 'sayer' and 'what is said'):

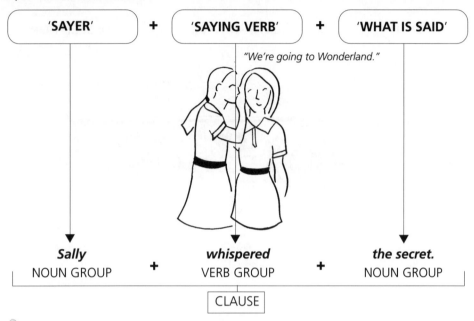

| 'SAYER' | + | 'SAYING VERB' | + | 'WHAT IS SAID' |

"We're going to Wonderland."

| **Sally** | + | **whispered** | + | **the secret.** |
| NOUN GROUP | | VERB GROUP | | NOUN GROUP |

CLAUSE

👁 Clauses with sensing verbs

When we talk about sensing verbs, we usually need to include the person who is doing the thinking, feeling or perceiving (the 'senser'). We often also refer to what the person is thinking, or feeling, or perceiving ('what is sensed'):

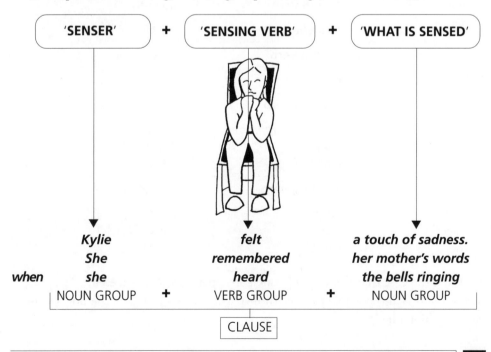

| 'SENSER' | + | 'SENSING VERB' | + | 'WHAT IS SENSED' |

	Kylie		**felt**		**a touch of sadness.**
	She		**remembered**		**her mother's words**
when	**she**		**heard**		**the bells ringing**
	NOUN GROUP	+	VERB GROUP	+	NOUN GROUP

CLAUSE

Clauses with relating verbs

We use relating verbs to make the link between someone or something (the 'entity') and some related information (the 'description'):

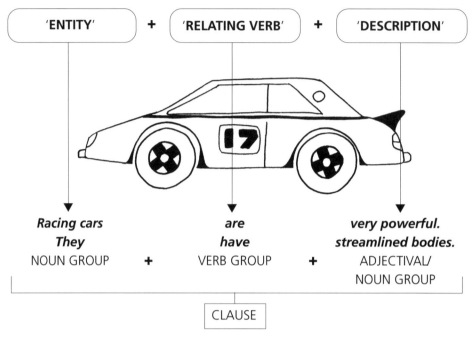

| 'ENTITY' | + | 'RELATING VERB' | + | 'DESCRIPTION' |

Racing cars		*are*		*very powerful.*
They		*have*		*streamlined bodies.*
NOUN GROUP	+	VERB GROUP	+	ADJECTIVAL/ NOUN GROUP

CLAUSE

Summary

We could summarise these different clause patterns as follows:

do-er	**Action verb**	done-to
The cat	*scratched*	*my hand.*
sayer	**Saying verb**	what is said
I	*muttered*	*my apologies.*
senser	**Sensing verb**	what is sensed
We	*couldn't remember*	*the plan.*
They	*love*	*Thai food.*
She	*wanted*	*a hug.*
entity	**Relating verb**	description
Spiders	*have*	*eight legs.*
They	*are*	*arachnids.*
They	*can be*	*poisonous.*

It is often the case that there is only one participant (eg '**She** sneezed.' '**They** laughed.'). It is also possible to have three participants ('**Jim** gave **the dog a bone.**' '**She** told **him a lie.**')

Interacting through clauses

While the above descriptions of clauses relate to how they function to represent the world and our experience in different ways, we can also look at clauses in terms of how they enable us to interact with each other.

Different types of clauses do different jobs in terms of facilitating interaction:

- we can simply state something (**statement**)
- or we can request information (**question**)
- or we can ask someone to do something (**command**)
- or we can express our feelings in an emphatic way (**exclamation**).

Statements

👁 *Looking at meaning*

We use statements to provide information, make remarks and assertions, and so on:

Silk is one of the strongest, most flexible materials produced in the natural world.
Shelley sulked all afternoon.
Once there was a man and his donkey.

Most written texts and oral presentations consist mainly of statements, unless there is a deliberate effort to interact with the audience.

🔧 *Formation*

The key elements in the structure of a statement are the subject followed by the auxiliary verb:

She	**has**	answered the phone.
SUBJECT	AUXILIARY	

They	**will**	leave at 8 o'clock.
SUBJECT	AUXILIARY	

Questions

👁 *Looking at meaning*

We use questions to enquire about something, to request information, to probe, and so on.

Are you okay?
Do you know Mary's last name?
How do you get to Marrickville from here?
What is it like to be old?

It is through asking questions that we stimulate interaction. Questions are used primarily in oral conversation, though you will also find them in written texts (such as in the dialogue sections of a story).

 Formation

When we look at the structure of a question, we notice that the auxiliary now comes in front of the subject (and, of course, a question mark is added):

Has	**she**	answered the phone?
AUXILIARY	SUBJECT	

Will	**they**	leave at 8 o'clock?
AUXILIARY	SUBJECT	

But what happens if there is no auxiliary (as with the present simple and past simple)? In that case, we need to 'invent' one by using 'do/does' or 'did':

She likes pasta. ➤ She **does** like pasta. ➤ **Does** she like pasta?
They went to Wagga. ➤ They **did** go to Wagga. ➤ **Did** they go to Wagga?

Sometimes we simply use a rising intonation to ask a question:

She likes pasta?

When we want confirmation, we can use a 'tag question':

She likes pasta, doesn't she?

> ### Troubleshooting
> *It is not important to teach the structure of questions as most students will be using them quite comfortably without explicit instruction. ESL students, however, often have problems with the structure of questions, and you might need to be able to explain how we construct them in English.*

The type of question above is generally called a 'yes/no' question. We can also ask 'wh-' questions: 'who?', 'when?', 'where?', and so on. These have a somewhat different structure and function. They still ask for information, but require an answer which goes beyond a simple 'yes' or 'no'. Certain types of 'wh-' questions (eg 'why?' and 'how?') are more demanding again, often requiring a lengthier, more complex response:

QUESTION TYPE	QUESTION	RESPONSE
'yes/no'	**Did they** go to Wagga?	Yes.
'wh–' (closed)	When **did they** leave?	At 8 o'clock.
'wh–' (open)	Why **did they** go?	Because John's father was sick and they wanted to see how he was going.

It is important that students are given opportunities not only to answer questions but to use and reflect on a range of question types, eg in morning news, class discussions, interviews, with guest speakers, and so on.

Commands

👁 *Looking at meaning*

We use commands to get things done, to obtain goods or services, and so on:

Pass the salt, please.
Tell me his name!
Place the mixture in the oven.

Commands are usually used in oral interaction, though they can be found in written procedures (such as instructions) or in dialogue.

🔲 *Formation*

The typical structure of a command is quite simple—we drop the subject and the auxiliary and just use the main verb:

Answer the phone.
Leave at 8 o'clock.

While this may be the most typical way of giving a command, we often use other structures when we want someone to do something. If we want to be polite or make a gentle request, we might use a question as a command:

Will you get me a cup of tea?
Would you mind closing the door?
Could you answer the phone?

Or we can make a statement which implies a request:

You might like to hold that for me.
The phone's ringing.

Young students are often not familiar with the more subtle ways in which we can make suggestions, requests and demands in English. They might be interested in exploring this area of grammar in relation to real life situations.

Exclamations

👁 *Looking at meaning*

We use exclamations to express surprise or make an emphatic statement:

How strange!
What a dill I am!

Students can explore different ways of using emphasis, stress and emotion in their oral and written language—particularly in dramatic presentations, stories, poems—including how it can be used for sarcasm and irony.

⊞ *Formation*

Sometimes we omit the verb altogether and use an expression such as
'How + adjectival!' or 'What + noun group!':

> How exciting!
> How hot it is!
> What a surprise!
> What idiots!

An exclamation mark is generally used to show that a statement is being used as
an exclamation:

> He's so generous!
> We had a great time!

Summary: Resources for interaction

The following is an excerpt from *Young Engineer in the Home* which seeks to engage
the reader in exploring the construction of houses. Look at how the writer has
employed statements, questions and commands when interacting with the reader.

Now go inside your house.	COMMAND
How many rooms are there?	QUESTION
Are they all the same shape and size?	QUESTION
If you have a loft, have a look up there.	COMMAND
Be careful though	COMMAND
and take an adult with you.	COMMAND
Can you see the rafters in the loft?	QUESTION
These help to keep up the ceilings.	STATEMENT
Can you see the struts?	QUESTION
These help to support the roof.	STATEMENT

Graham Weston

Early Primary

Learning to ...

In their oral language, most students will be using a full range of clause patterns. Some of their statements may lack agreement between subject and verb. They will be using several different types of clauses (statements, questions, commands and exclamations), though some students (particularly of ESL background) might have trouble forming questions correctly. In their writing, they will tend to use simple statements. Sometimes their writing will take the form of a 'sentence fragment' (eg omitting the verb).

Learning about ...

In their discussions, writing, reading and viewing, students can be guided to notice the different functions of statements, questions, commands, and exclamations. When exploring what is happening in a text, they should be able to recognise and talk about the components of simple clauses involving action verbs ('do-er' + 'action verb' + 'done-to') and saying verbs ('sayer' + 'saying verb' + 'what is said'). They might be starting to recognise clauses as meaningful chunks: 'a group of words which tell us about an action and those involved in the action', though they may not yet be using the word 'clause'.

Mid Primary

Learning to ...

Most students should be comprehending and employing a wide variety of clause types in their oral language. In the written mode it is more likely that they will be using statements, with a few questions, commands and exclamations in their narratives (particularly in the dialogue). In terms of structure, their use of syntax in written texts should be relatively accurate.

Learning about ...

Students might start looking at the syntax of clauses if this is felt to be useful (eg subject/verb/object), particularly in terms of agreement between subject and verb. When considering the meaning of different types of clauses, students might look at the different components of clauses involving sensing verbs (eg 'senser' + 'sensing verb' + 'what is sensed'—or more particularly, for example, 'thinker' + 'thinking verb' + 'what is thought') and might explore how these contribute to the meaning of the text. They might examine clauses involving relating verbs ('entity' + 'relating verb' + 'description') and the function of such clauses (eg describing, defining, classifying, indicating attributes). Students could investigate different types of questions (eg yes/no, open, closed) and commands (eg direct and indirect) and see how these relate to the situation in which they are being used (eg in terms of status, power, authority, age) — who is asking the questions? what type? who is giving the commands? in what way?

Later Primary

Learning to ...

Students should be able to create a variety of well-structured clauses in both their talking and writing. They should be able to manipulate the clause patterns when necessary in order to achieve particular effects. In their reading, they should comprehend the clause as a meaningful unit and recognise the main components of the clause as significant 'chunks'.

Learning about ...

Students might reflect on the different types of clauses in a text and how these contribute to the meaning of the text (eg who is doing the action? who is being affected by the action? who is the initiator? who is playing a more passive role? who does all the talking? why? what sort of things are being said? why is the writer telling us about the thoughts/feelings of a particular character? what does this tell us about the character? at what point in a story might we expect to hear about thoughts and feelings? why does a narrative contain the full range of clause types while procedures have mainly clauses involving action verbs?) In particular, the notion of active and passive could be introduced, perhaps within the context of media studies. In terms of structure, some students (particularly ESL students and those learning a LOTE) might benefit from learning about direct and indirect objects.

Combining clauses

So far we have been working at the level of the clause and below the clause (groups and words). It is often the case, however, that clauses are combined in various ways to produce different types of sentences. Here we will look at a range of sentence types.

Simple sentences

 *Formation*

A simple sentence is one which contains a single clause. Most of the sentences we have been dealing with so far have been simple sentences, eg:

> We had a great time!
> Could you answer the phone?
> They went to Wagga.
> I muttered my apologies.

A clause which can stand on its own is called an **independent** (or main/principal) clause.

Combined clauses

Many sentences, however, contain more than one clause—sometimes as many as four or five (and more!), eg:

> Possum found a safe tree
> and climbed to the farthest branches
> where he snuggled into a ball,
> closed his weary eyes
> and fell asleep.

We can combine clauses in different ways to make different types of sentences:

- compound sentences
- complex sentences, and
- compound/complex sentences

Compound sentences

 ### *Formation*

Compound sentences consist of two or more independent clauses. Each of these clauses is capable of standing on its own and conveying a message. Each has equal status and provides equally important information. These clauses may be linked together in a sentence using such words as 'and', 'or', 'but', eg:

He climbed into bed	INDEPENDENT CLAUSE
and he fell fast asleep.	INDEPENDENT CLAUSE
Susan walked home	INDEPENDENT CLAUSE
but the others caught the bus.	INDEPENDENT CLAUSE
You could ring him at work	INDEPENDENT CLAUSE
or you could try him at home.	INDEPENDENT CLAUSE

Words used to combine independent clauses include:

and	so	either … or
but	and so	neither … nor
or	and then	not only … but also

 ### *Looking at meaning*

Young children tend to rely more heavily on compound sentences (though they are quite capable of using more complex sentences, particularly in their oral language). Recount texts in particular typically consist of a string of independent clauses joined by 'and' and 'then'. Simple information reports often consist of a number of factual statements joined by 'and'. As students learn to express thoughts with more complex relationships they will need to use complex sentences.

Complex sentences

 ### *Formation*

In a **complex sentence**, there is a clause expressing the main message and another clause (or clauses) which elaborates on that message in some way. While the main clause is independent, the other clause cannot stand on its own—it is **dependent** on the main clause for its meaning.

They ran	INDEPENDENT CLAUSE
as if they were being chased by a madman.	DEPENDENT CLAUSE
The metal rod expanded	INDEPENDENT CLAUSE
because it was heated.	DEPENDENT CLAUSE
If the box breaks	DEPENDENT CLAUSE
the beads will spill everywhere.	INDEPENDENT CLAUSE

Dependent clauses are sometimes called **adverbial clauses** because they often perform a job similar to adverbs and adverbial phrases, providing more information about 'how', 'when', 'where', 'why' and so on. They can also be called **subordinate clauses**.

Sometimes complex sentences involve clauses which don't contain a full (or **finite**) verb, eg:

You can get immediate help	INDEPENDENT CLAUSE
by **dialling** the emergency number.	DEPENDENT CLAUSE—NON-FINITE
To make vegetable soup,	DEPENDENT CLAUSE—NON-FINITE
you will need a clear broth.	INDEPENDENT CLAUSE

A non-finite verb does not have a subject. Generally, you can 'translate' a non-finite verb in a dependent clause into its finite form, eg:

They crawled to the top of the hill to **see** *[non-finite]* the surrounding landscape.
They crawled to the top of the hill so that **they could see** *[finite]* the surrounding landscape.

Sitting *[non-finite]* alone in her bedroom, she began to think of what had happened.
As she sat *[finite]* alone in her bedroom, she began to think of what had happened.

◉ *Looking at meaning*

Complex sentences generally involve greater complexity of thought as students learn to express more subtle and intricate relationships between ideas. They are often used, for example, to convey the logical reasoning needed in argumentation and explanation.

> ### *Troubleshooting*
>
> *Apart from learning to express logical relationships in their writing, students also need to be able to comprehend such relationships in their reading. Research indicates that many students don't fully recognise these relationships and therefore have difficulty in following the meaning of the text. It has been found for example that the conditional 'if' is understood by only fifty per cent of children at age six; that the meaning of 'unless' is often not understood well until after the age of nine; and it is generally not until around twelve years of age that many children comprehend the concessive use of 'although'.*

Compound/complex sentences

 *Formation*

Some sentences contain a combination of independent and dependent clauses.
These can be referred to as compound/complex sentences, eg:

Two kookaburras flew into the tree	INDEPENDENT CLAUSE
and cackled loudly	INDEPENDENT CLAUSE
as they scanned the nearby bush for food.	DEPENDENT CLAUSE
A gunman died of massive head wounds today	INDEPENDENT CLAUSE
after shooting his estranged wife	DEPENDENT CLAUSE
and injuring two other people.	DEPENDENT CLAUSE

Conjunctions

Conjunctions are used to link dependent clauses and independent clauses.
Different types of conjunctions are used to express different types of relationships
between ideas. The following chart gives an indication of the ways in which
conjunctions can be used.

	CONJUNCTIONS	**EXAMPLE**
Place	where, wherever	***Wherever I go*** *I meet my relatives.* *She left it **where she found it**.*
Time *WHEN?*	after, before, when, just as, as, while	*He realised he had lost it **when he arrived home**.* ***Before I decide**, I want to talk to Harry.*
HOW LONG?	as long as, since, until, while	*I haven't seen her **since she moved to Dubbo**.* ***Until the rash clears up** you will have to stay at home.*
HOW OFTEN?	whenever, every time	*I get goosebumps **whenever I hear him**.* ***Every time she rings up** I pretend I'm not home.*
Manner *QUALITY*	the way that, as	***The way she spends money** you'd think she'd won Lotto.*
MEANS	by, through, with	***By working overtime** she managed to finish the project.*
COMPARISON	as if, as though, as, like, the way	*I couldn't lie **like he does**.* *She looked **as if she needed a good rest**.*
Cause *REASON*	as, because, since, seeing that, in case	*I came **because he called me**.* ***Since you obviously aren't interested**, let's leave it.*
PURPOSE	so that, in order to, so as to, in order that	*They went outside **to see what the noise was**.* *We left early **so that we could get a parking space**.*
RESULT	so … that, such a(n) … that	*We were **so** tired **that we couldn't stay awake**.* *It was **such** a rainy night **that we decided to stay home**.*
Condition	as long as, if, in case, unless, on condition that	*Never sit on a nest of ants **unless you're wearing cast-iron pants**.* ***If she wants to come** she'll have to hurry up.*
Concession	although, even though, even if, while, whereas, despite, much as	***Even though they weren't hungry**, they ate a full meal.* ***While recognising his skill**, I don't think he is right for the job.*

Relative clauses

We have already met relative (or adjectival) clauses when we were looking at the noun group (eg '**The woman I met at the party** is Sarah's grandmother.'). These are another type of dependent clause, but rather than provide more information about the verb (as with adverbial clauses) they provide more information about the noun.

Quoting and reporting

There is another way in which we can combine messages. When we use saying verbs and sensing verbs, we often include a clause (or clauses) indicating what was said or sensed.

Quoting

 **Formation**

In some cases, we quote the actual words said or thought, eg:

"What's the matter?"	QUOTED CLAUSE (actual words)
asked Andrew.	QUOTING CLAUSE
The girl cried:	QUOTING CLAUSE
"Apple tree, please hide us!"	QUOTED CLAUSE (actual words)
"Eat one of my crab-apples,"	QUOTED CLAUSE (actual words)
the tree answered,	QUOTING CLAUSE
"and I will tell you."	QUOTED CLAUSE (actual words)
'There is nothing to worry about,'	QUOTED CLAUSE (actual words)
Maria thought to herself.	QUOTING CLAUSE

This is often referred to as **direct speech**.

Reporting

 **Formation**

Rather than quoting the exact words, we sometimes report what was said or thought, eg:

I told him	REPORTING CLAUSE
that I was sorry.	REPORTED CLAUSE
She said	REPORTING CLAUSE
she never wanted to see him again.	REPORTED CLAUSE
They thought	REPORTING CLAUSE
it was rather odd.	REPORTED CLAUSE

This is called **indirect speech**.

👁 *Looking at meaning*

Both quoting and reporting are found in text types such as newspaper articles, stories, advertisements, biographies and recounts.

In terms of meaning, students might be encouraged to think about why a writer would choose either to use a direct quote or to report indirectly what has been said. They might also reflect on how quoting and reporting on what characters say, think and feel in a narrative can help build up the character and give insights into their motivations, reflections, intentions, desires, and so on. When reading and writing expository texts, students might discuss such issues as when it is appropriate to quote someone, why you would select a particular authority to quote, how quoting can add weight to an argument, the difference between citing, paraphrasing, and plagiarising.

Structuring sentences

A major skill which primary students need to develop is how to create well-structured sentences. Student texts often sound awkward because of the over-use of simple (single-clause) sentences or because of the use of long, rambling, incoherent sentences.

Simple sentences are quite appropriate (and indeed functional) in text types such as procedures. They are short, uncluttered and 'to the point'. They are also effective when used at particular stages in a story—to disrupt the rhythm, to introduce a staccato effect or to make a significant point.

Longer sentences are also appropriate when there are a number of closely related ideas which need to be brought together. These sentences generally require careful crafting, however, and students need to be aware of the various ways in which information can be presented and clauses can be combined.

In written texts, we tend to pack more information into the clause by extending the noun group. Look at the following text by a Year 1 student:

> There was an elephant.
> His name was Ahmed.
> He was big.
> He was also old.
> And he had long tusks.

This information could have been combined into a single clause by building up the noun group:

> Ahmed was **a big, old elephant with long tusks**.

Other texts, especially recounts and stories, often end up as a long string of clauses:

One day I was playing with my friends
and I saw a ghost
and it was flying towards me
so I ran as fast as I could
but then it disappeared
then it appeared again
so I ran for home
then the ghost went through the wall
then I went to my bedroom
but the ghost went through my bedroom door
then I woke up
and it was all a dream.

Apart from working on the development of this story, the student needs help with combining clauses into distinct sentences, eg:

One day, when I was playing with my friends, I saw a ghost flying towards me. I ran as fast as I could but then it disappeared. (Suddenly) it appeared again so I ran for home. But the ghost went through the wall. I went to my bedroom but the ghost went through my bedroom door. Then I woke up (to find) it was all a dream.

Troubleshooting

The above weaknesses are common in younger students' writing and many will learn how to construct more satisfactory texts as they gain more experience through reading and writing. There are many older students, however, who still have trouble structuring coherent, well-balanced sentences and who need explicit assistance in such matters as how to:

- *build up the noun group*
- *combine information by using adjectival phrases and adjectival clauses*
- *most effectively use simple sentences*
- *combine clauses in a variety of ways*
- *develop compound sentences, complex sentences and compound/complex sentences*
- *use parentheses, colons and dashes to elaborate*
- *use quoting and reporting sentences.*

Combining clauses: Development through the stages

Early Primary

Learning to ...

Most students will quite comfortably use and comprehend relatively lengthy compound sentences when speaking and listening (although when speaking to some students, the relationship signalled by certain conjunctions might need to be emphasised). They will be able to understand stories read to them which employ a variety of clause combinations. Students' written texts (especially recounts and stories) often tend to resemble spoken language, with several clauses strung together with 'and', 'then' and 'but'.

Learning about ...

In their writing and reading, students should be made aware of sentence boundaries. When reading to students, teachers can model the 'meaning units' (clauses) within sentences through intonation and pausing. Their attention may be drawn to the length of sentences, the number of ideas contained within a sentence, and the punctuation signalling the beginning and end of a sentence. In relation to students' writing, attention could be paid to dividing long rambling sentences into shorter sentences of two or three clauses.

Mid Primary

Learning to ...

Most students should be comprehending and employing a wide variety of sentence types (compound, complex, compound/complex, as well as quoting and reporting sentences) in both their spoken and written language. Sentences in their written texts might still be overly long and rambling, overly short and stilted, awkwardly structured, or poorly punctuated. In their reading, students should be exposed to texts which provide models of richly patterned sentences. If a class text proves to be daunting, students should be introduced to strategies for 'unpacking' the text (eg seeing it in terms of 'meaning units', identifying the relationship between units/clauses, unravelling lengthy noun groups).

Learning about ...

Students should be able to identify basic examples of clauses within a sentence and to discuss how these are typically joined together with conjunctions ('joining words'). Attention should be drawn to ways of improving poorly structured sentences. Students should be learning how to use quoting and reporting (direct and indirect speech) and how to punctuate quoted speech and thoughts. They might discuss when and why you would choose to use quoting and reporting.

Later Primary

Learning to ...

By now students' written texts (and prepared oral presentations) should be differentiated from their more spontaneous spoken language, demonstrating a more crafted, compact quality. Careful and informed reworking of sentences should be a regular feature of their writing practices (including relevant aspects of punctuation: commas, semicolons, colons, dashes, parentheses). There should be evidence of students using a wide range of dependent clauses (eg place, time, manner, cause, condition, concession) appropriately in terms of the type of text being written. Dependent clauses may include either finite or non-finite verbs. Quoting and reporting sentences should be used effectively, with accurate punctuation, in texts such as stories, biographies, historical recounts, and exposition.

Learning about ...

Students should be able to identify, in broad terms, different types of sentences (simple, compound, complex and compound/complex) and to recognise different types of relationships between clauses as signalled by conjunctions. They should be able to reflect on and discuss the selection of different sentence types in terms of how they contribute to the impact and flow of the text. They should be aware of the difference between quoting, reporting, paraphrasing and plagiarism. They should be learning how to cite an author in an expository text and provide an adequate reference.

Text level

So far, we have looked at language structures and features at the word level, the group level, the clause level and the sentence level. We can now go further and see how language operates at the level of the text.

Text organisation

Text structure

Each text type is structured in a particular way to achieve its purpose. A recount, for example, will generally begin with an Orientation stage in which the various participants are introduced and the time and setting clarified. This is followed by a Record of Events, outlining what happened in chronological order. An exposition, on the other hand, will typically begin with a Thesis, stating the position being argued for. This will be followed by a series of Arguments which are brought together in the Conclusion.

The various ways in which text types are structured have been described elsewhere, for example *Exploring How Texts Work* (PETA 1990) and *Teaching About Texts* (NSW Board of Studies 1999).

Paragraphs

One thing which adds to the coherence of a text is the way we divide it into **paragraphs**. The author needs to decide how to divide the written material into manageable and logical 'bundles', each of which deals with a single, unified topic or event. The length of a paragraph can range from an individual sentence through to a number of sentences. Paragraphs help the reader to discern the major points being made in the text and the shifts between those points.

Topic sentences

A paragraph generally contains a **topic sentence**. This generally occurs at the beginning of the paragraph and summarises the main point being made in the paragraph. It is often a relatively general statement, which is followed up in the rest of the paragraph with various elaborations such as examples, definitions, description, supporting evidence, and so on—depending on the purpose of the text.

Theme

At the more micro-level, the flow of information in the text is controlled by the choice of theme. The technical term 'theme' refers to the beginning of the clause. At the text level, the beginnings of the clauses focus our attention on how the topic is being developed. This helps to make the text coherent and to enable the reader to predict how the text is unfolding.

👁 Looking at meaning

Let's look at the above features in a descriptive text about the city of New York:

> **New York** is a city of things unnoticed. **It** is a city with cats sleeping under parked cars, two stone armadillos crawling up St Patrick's Cathedral, and thousands of ants creeping on top of the Empire State Building. …
>
> **Some of New York's best informed men** are elevator operators, who rarely talk, but always listen — like doormen. **Sardi's doormen** listen to the comments made by Broadway's first-nighters walking by after the last act. **They** listen closely. **They** listen carefully. **They** can tell you within ten minutes which shows will flop and which will be hits. …
>
> **New York** is a town of 3,000 bootblacks whose brushes and rhythmic rag-snaps can be heard up and down Manhattan from midmorning to midnight. **They** dodge cops, survive rainstorms, and thrive in the Empire State Building as well as on the Staten Island Ferry. **They** usually wear dirty shoes. …
>
> *G. Talese*

The text is divided up into **paragraphs**, each dealing with a particular aspect of the topic.

Each paragraph begins with a **topic sentence** (underlined above).

- The first topic sentence—New York is a city of things unnoticed.—is then exemplified in the rest of the paragraph with various types of unnoticed things: cats, stone armadillos, and ants. This topic sentence also acts as an organiser for the whole text, each paragraph of which elaborates on all the unnoticed things which inhabit the city.

- The second paragraph begins with the topic sentence —Some of New York's best informed men are elevator operators, who rarely talk, but always listen—*like doormen.*— which is elaborated on with an example of how Sardi's doormen (another of New York's 'unnoticed') listen intently to the first-nighters.

- The topic sentence of the third paragraph—New York is a town of 3,000 bootblacks whose brushes and rhythmic rag-snaps can be heard up and down Manhattan from midmorning to midnight.—introduces another of New York's silent inhabitants, the bootblacks, who are then described in the following sentences.

The beginning of each sentence or **theme** (in bold in the text) alerts us to the topic which is being developed, while the end of the sentence introduces the new information about the topic.

- In the first paragraph, the theme is **New York** and this is picked up as the theme of the following sentence.

- In the second paragraph, the theme is **Some of New York's best informed men**, which becomes more specific ('Sardi's doormen'), who are then picked up as 'they'.

- The theme of the third paragraph starts off as **New York,** but then changes to the **bootblacks** who have just been introduced. The theme then follows through the bootblacks for the rest of the paragraph. This is a typical theme pattern for descriptions and information reports, but not necessarily for other text types.

THEME	NEW INFORMATION
New York ↓	is a city of things unnoticed.
It	is a city with cats sleeping under parked cars, two stone armadillos crawling up St Patrick's Cathedral, and thousands of ants creeping on top of the Empire State Building.
Some of New York's best informed men	are elevator operators, who rarely talk, but always listen—like <u>doormen</u>.
Sardi's doormen ↓	listen to the comments made by Broadway's first-nighters walking by after the last act.
They ↓	listen closely.
They ↓	listen carefully.
They	can tell you within ten minutes which shows will flop and which will be hits.
New York	is a town of <u>3,000 bootblacks</u> whose brushes and rhythmic rag-snaps can be heard up and down Manhattan from midmorning to midnight.
They	dodge cops, survive rainstorms, and thrive in the Empire State Building as well as on the Staten Island Ferry.
They	usually wear dirty shoes.

This type of pattern adds to the predictability of texts, making them easier to read and familiarising students with the need to focus on the beginning of the clause to get an idea of the 'theme' and on the end for the new information.

There are a number of possible theme patterns which a writer can draw upon in writing a text:

- in a recount the writer might use the beginning of the clause to develop the timeline, eg

  'In 1968 ...', 'Later on ...', 'In the early 70's ...', 'Soon after ...'.

- in a procedure the beginning focus is generally on the sequence of actions which need to be carried out, eg

  'Pour ...', 'Mix ...', 'Stir ...', 'Bake ...'.

- in an exposition, the beginning of the clause is often used to structure the argument, eg

  'Firstly ...', 'However ...', 'In conclusion ...'.

- Sometimes, particularly in literary texts such as narratives and poems, the writer might want to unsettle the reader or to highlight the unusual. This often involves making an unexpected choice of theme, eg:

Slobbering and foolish, the young retriever dog jumped excitedly all over them.
Stimulated by the crisis, Andy's brain began to work.
Down came a jumbuck to drink at the water-hole,
Up jumped the swagman and grabbed him with glee.

These are stylistic decisions which the author has made in order to arouse interest and focus on a particular aspect. Young writers might be encouraged to find examples of such uses and to reflect on the effect of making different choices in theme position.

Troubleshooting

It is careful attention to theme which makes a text more coherent and considerate towards the reader. The theme signals to the reader 'This is what I want you to pay attention to' ... 'Now I'm shifting my focus' ... 'Now I want you to attend to this' ... 'Now I'm introducing another aspect of the theme' ... and so on.

Some young writers' texts sound awkward and poorly structured because they have not thought about how to guide the reader through the text by using the beginning of the clause as a signpost.

Cohesion

At the text level, there are a number of other devices we can use to organise a text so that it is cohesive and coherent. These cohesive devices make links between various items in the text so that the reader is able to 'track' how the meaning is being developed.

Referring words

One way in which we can set up links in a text is to use words which refer back to something which has already been mentioned. The most common of these cohesive devices are the **pronouns**:

Terry was drifting off to sleep when [he] heard a strange noise.

In the following story, we can see how the pronouns keep referring back to the main character, the Jackdaw. There are also minor reference links to the Peacocks and to the Jackdaw's former companions.

THE VAIN JACKDAW

A vain Jackdaw, tired of [his] drab plumage, was envious of

the brilliant colours of the Peacock. [He] picked up some of

the feathers which the Peacocks had shed along the bank of the river,

stuck them amongst [his] own, and admired [his] reflection in the water.

Despising [his] old companions, [he] introduced [himself] to a flock of

those beautiful birds. [**They,**] instantly detecting the intruder,

stripped [him] of [his] borrowed plumes, and falling upon [him] with

[**their**] beaks and claws, sent [him] about [his] business.

The humbled Jackdaw, sorely punished and deeply sorrowing,

took [himself] off to [***his***] ***former companions***, hoping to rejoin

[his] old flock as if nothing had happened. But [**they,**] recollecting how

conceited [he] was, drummed [him] out of [***their***] society, admonishing

[him] that if [he] had been contented with what nature made [him,] [he] would

have escaped the chastisement of [his] betters and the contempt of [his] equals.

Aesop

Other referring words include:

- **the definite article** ('the') when it is used to refer back to something which has been introduced previously and which we can now take for granted:

  <u>A</u> vain Jackdaw … **The** humbled Jackdaw …

- words which replace verb groups or noun groups or even whole clauses (eg 'do', 'so', 'such', 'one'):

  'I told him <u>to leave</u>. And he **did**.'
  'I've two <u>umbrellas</u>. Would you like **one**?'
  '<u>She was very tired</u>.' 'Yes, I thought **so**.'

- the pointing words 'this', 'that', 'these' and 'those'

  The water vapour cools and condenses into clouds of <u>droplets</u>.
  These fall as rain on land and sea.

  <u>Trees absorb carbon dioxide from the atmosphere and use it to make starch for food</u>. **This** is called photosynthesis.

Word associations

Another way in which links are set up within a text is through word associations, eg

- repetition
- synonyms
- antonyms
- collocation
- word sets (class/subclass; part/whole)

In the text above, certain words (eg Jackdaw) are **repeated**. This is the most simple kind of cohesion, where we can easily track the participants because they are referred to using the same word through the text.

A less direct way of forming a link is to use **synonyms** (ie words which have a similar meaning). In the above text, the Jackdaw is also referred to as 'the intruder', while the Peacocks are called 'those beautiful birds' and 'his betters'. The birds' plumage is also referred to as 'feathers' and 'plumes'. On the one hand, this adds interest and subtlety to the text, but on the other hand it can make it difficult for inexperienced readers and ESL students to track the participants.

Similarly, **antonyms** can be used to create a different type of link. Antonyms are opposite in meaning rather than similar. In the text, for example, we find 'his drab plumage' contrasted with 'the brilliant colours' of the Peacocks. There is also the contrast between 'a vain Jackdaw' and 'the humbled Jackdaw'.

Collocation is a term used for words which typically occur together, making a text predictable. In the above text, for example, we find 'river', 'bank', 'water' and 'reflection'.

Word sets are particular 'clusters' of words in a text which are related in various ways. They might be related in terms of 'whole' and 'part', such as the body parts of the Peacocks:

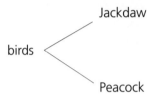

Or they might be related in terms of 'class' and 'subclass'. While this is more common in information reports, there is mention in this text of two classes of birds:

birds < Jackdaw / Peacock

Or the relationship might be in terms of a thing and its attributes, such as in the description of the Jackdaw:

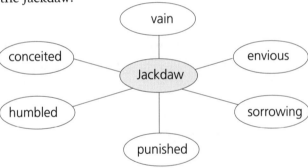

If we want to trace the development of the main participants in a text, we can draw up 'word chains' by noting the various ways in which they are mentioned in the text:

the Jackdaw	**his companions**	**the Peacocks**
a vain Jackdaw	his old companions	the brilliant colours
drab plumage	his former companions	the Peacock
his reflection	his old flock	feathers
the intruder	their society	the Peacocks
his borrowed plumes	his equals	a flock
the humbled Jackdaw		those beautiful birds
		beaks
		claws
		his betters

In literary texts in particular, we can also create links by using **similes, metaphors** and **'allusion'**. Aesop could have described the peacock feathers, for example, as being 'like emeralds' (simile), setting up a relationship between the green of the feathers and the green of an emerald. Or he could have said that the Peacocks were 'aristocrats' (metaphor), conjuring up in the reader's mind all the images associated with aristocracy. Another way of creating links beyond the text itself is to use 'allusion', where the writer enriches a text by making indirect reference to other texts. In the above fable, for example, the line 'admired his reflection in the water' brings to mind the story of Narcissus, thereby drawing a parallel between the two texts.

Text connectives

Other words which contribute to the cohesion of the text are the **text connectives**. These are often called 'connectors', 'discourse markers' or 'signal words'. They provide the reader with signposts indicating how the text is developing. If the writer wants to show that a summary is coming up, for example, a phrase such as 'In short ...' or 'Briefly ...' can be used. If the text is giving a sequence of points, these can be highlighted by the use of such words as 'To begin ...', 'Secondly ...', 'In conclusion ...'.

The following is a list of commonly used text connectives:

Clarifying	Showing cause/result	Indicating time
in other words	so	then
I mean	therefore	next
to put it another way	then	afterwards
for example	consequently	at the same time
for instance	in/as a consequence	before that
to be more precise	as a result	in the end
or rather	for that reason	finally
in particular	due to ..., owing to ...	soon
in fact	accordingly	after a while
as a matter of fact	because of this	at this point
that is	in that case	meanwhile
namely		at this moment
to illustrate		later
		previously
		earlier
		until then

Sequencing ideas	Adding information	Condition/concession
firstly, first	too	in that case
in the first place	in addition	otherwise
first of all	indeed	if not
to start with	apart from that	however
to begin	also	nevertheless
for a start	furthermore	despite this
second, third, fourth ...	on top of that	besides
at this point	and besides	yet
to get back to the point	above all	on the other hand
then	along with	however
in short	what's more	on the contrary
all in all	again	anyhow, anyway
briefly	let alone	instead
to summarise/to sum up	as well	still
finally	likewise	even so
a final point	moreover	all the same
to conclude	similarly	in any case
in conclusion	equally	at least
given the above points	in the same way	though
in light of the above		despite this

Troubleshooting

Sometimes text <u>connectives</u> are confused with <u>conjunctions</u>, and indeed they often perform a very similar function. Conjunctions, however, join two clauses and only operate within a sentence. Text connectives, on the other hand, form links between sentences and other longer stretches of text. Also, while conjunctions are placed at the beginning of a clause, text connectives can be more freely placed at various positions within the sentence (as, for example, in the use of 'however' and 'on the other hand' in this paragraph).

All the cohesive devices above set up different types of links in the text, weaving a tapestry of meaning for the reader to perceive and appreciate. Students need to be able to create these patterns in their own writing with increasing sophistication and need to be able to decode the cohesive links when reading texts—a skill not fully developed until adulthood.

Grammatical patterns

Each text type will also have certain grammatical patterns typically associated with it which help to develop the kinds of meanings generally associated with that text-type. Knowing about these patterns can help us to focus on particular features when working with the class.

👁 *Looking at meaning*

The sorts of questions we could ask about a text might include:

What kinds of *nouns* might we find in this text?

- living/non-living?
- human/non-human?
- masculine/feminine/neuter?
- proper/common?
- particular/general?
- concrete/abstract?
- everyday/technical?
- objective/subjective?

This gives us an indication of the subject-matter being developed in the text and the kind of knowledge being built up. Is the text concerned, for example, with participants which are non-living, general, technical and objective—such as an information report? Or are the participants living, human, gendered, particular, everyday beings—such as in a story?

What kinds of *adjectivals* might we find in this text?

- possessives?
- quantity adjectives?
- opinion adjectives?
- factual adjectives?
- comparing adjectives?
- classifying adjectives?

This will help us focus on the description in the text: quantities in a maths problem; persuasion in an exposition; objectivity in a factual recount; comparison in a description; classification in an information report; and so on.

What kinds of *pronouns* might we find in this text?

- personal pronouns?
- possessive pronouns?

We could ask how the pronouns are being used to develop relationships, eg between the speaker and listener, between the reader and writer, or between different participants in the text. Is the reader addressed as 'you'? Why/why not? Does the writer identify herself or himself as 'I'? What is the effect of this? Is 'we' used to include the audience? How are certain groups excluded by the use of the third person pronouns? Is possession an important issue in the text?

What kinds of *noun groups* might we find in this text?

- simple?
- complex?
- a mixture?

Here we could consider how well our students are exploiting the possibilites offered by the noun group. Are they sticking to simple, 'safe' noun groups? Are they using short, stark groups for a particular effect? Are they experimenting with longer groups containing a variety of adjectivals, such as building up the description in an information report? Are they learning to extend the noun group to include adjectival phrases and adjectival clauses? Are they able to comprehend more complex noun groups in their reading? Are their reading materials providing them with good, challenging models of complex noun groups? In which types of text are you more likely to find lengthy noun groups? Are they able to perceive a cluster of words as a noun group as opposed to a string of single items?

What kinds of *verbs* and *verb groups* might we find in this text?

- action verbs?
- saying verbs?
- sensing verbs?
- relating verbs?

Is the text concerned with actions, as in a recount or story? Is it concerned with what people are saying, as in a newspaper story or a narrative? Is it using direct or indirect speech? Why? Is it concerned with what people are sensing—their feelings, desires, thoughts, memories, hopes, regrets, opinions, beliefs—as in many stories, discussions and poems? Or is it concerned with linking bits of information, using relating verbs to describe, exemplify, classify, define, and so on, as in information reports and many maths problems?

What other information does the *verb group* contain?

- tense?
- modals?
- negative forms?

The verb groups in a text can also tell us about time, degree of commitment, and positive and negative aspects. Texts are generally located in a particular time frame (tense): is the text projecting into the future? is it about some specific event in the past? is it about regular, habitual actions in the past? is it presenting 'timeless' facts? Modality might be used to introduce an element of doubt or tentativeness or definiteness: is the writer trying to sound authoritative? does the speaker want to leave room for negotiation? is the text attempting to sound neutral? The use of negatives through the text can introduce a certain mood, where the writer or speaker is making judgements about a situation: 'I **dis**like skiing; I **never** have fun; I'm **not** going this year.'.

What kinds of *adverbials* might we find in this text?

- place (where?)
- time (when? how long? how often?)
- manner (in what way? by what means? like what?)
- cause (why?)
- accompaniment (with whom?)
- viewpoint and comment adverbials?
- degree adverbials?
- focusing and emphasising adverbials?

Certain text types (eg recounts, stories) will focus on adverbs and adverbial phrases which tell us when something happened, where it happened and in what manner. Text types such as procedures will rely on precise adverbials to provide such information as: how long? in which way? by what means? how frequently? Explanations and expositions might include adverbials of cause and reason. Some texts (eg stories and discussions) might present a particular point of view through viewpoint and comment adverbials.

What *patterns of clause organisation* might we find in this text?

- do-er + action verb + done-to?
- sayer + saying verb + what is said?
- senser + sensing verb + what is sensed?
- entity + relating verb + description?

By looking at the clause patterns in the text, we can get a feel for how the text is representing the world: who are the 'do-ers'? what sort of actions are they involved in? is anyone or anything generally more passive, in the 'done-to' role? Who is speaking in this text? Why are they chosen to speak? To whom are they speaking? What sorts of things are they saying? Are they being quoted directly or are they being paraphrased? What is the difference in effect? Are the characters portrayed as thinking and feeling beings? What insights do we get into their characters from what they are reported as thinking and feeling? How does this affect the story? What sort of relationship is being set up by the relating verbs (eg description? definition? classification?). Does any one type of verb predominate in the text? Are your students employing a variety of clause patterns as appropriate?

What *different types of clauses* might we find in this text?

- statements?
- questions?
- commands?
- exclamations?

In spoken language and in text types such as stories and recounts, we often find dialogue patterns consisting of various types of clauses which foster interaction between the participants: is the text simply a string of statements? Are any questions asked? How many? What kind? By whom? To whom? With what response? Who gives the commands? To whom? In what way? With what effect? How are turns taken? Who initiates a turn? Who changes the topic? Who interrupts? Who is supportive? In what way? How are communication breakdowns repaired?

What *different types of sentences* might we find in this text?

- simple sentences?
- compound sentences ?
- complex sentences?
- compound/complex sentences?

Certain texts, such as procedures, need to be very straightforward and easy to read. These texts tend to use simple sentences, consisting of a single clause (ie one message per sentence). Other texts need to use quite lengthy, complex sentences in order to develop a particular line of reasoning or to make certain connections. Many texts will use a combination of simple sentences and more complex sentences. If a text (including those written by students) consists mainly of simple (and perhaps compound) sentences, we might ask whether this is an effective way of presenting its message. If the text uses a number of lengthy, compound/complex sentences, we might ask whether this is appropriate, depending on the purpose and audience. If there is a mixture of sentence types throughout the text, what effect does this have? You could also look at the way in which the clauses are joined together with conjunctions: what type of relationship does the conjunction signal—time? reason? purpose? manner? and so on.

Which features contribute to the *organisation* of this text?

- text structure?
- paragraphs?
- topic sentences?
- theme?

Texts are structured in different ways according to their social purpose. A set of instructions, for example, is structured very differently from an argumentative essay. The instructions will probably contain a set of stages such as 'Goal' and 'Steps' while the essay might include stages such as 'Thesis', 'Arguments', and 'Conclusion'. Within these texts, paragraphs might be used in different ways to organise the information. Instructions will generally use very brief paragraphs, often consisting of a single, short sentence. An essay, on the other hand, might need some relatively lengthy paragraphs to develop the argumentation. The topic sentence of each paragraph might be quite obvious and placed at the beginning of the paragraph, as in most information reports. Or it might be buried and difficult to identify, as in many literary texts. The choice of theme (or 'sentence focus') will vary according to the type of text. In a procedure, the theme is typically a sequence of verbs giving a command. In an information report, the theme is typically the topic of the report (eg 'Marsupials'). In an historical recount, we find a number of adverbials as theme, sequencing the events in time

Which features contribute to the *cohesion* of this text?

- referring words?
- word associations?
- text connectives?

How are words like pronouns being used to make links within a text? Are these links easy to follow? Or might they be obscure, ambiguous or complex (eg when the referring word is quite distant from what it is referring to, or when a referring word such as 'this' is used to refer to a whole stretch of text)? What is the relationship between different ideas in the text? In an information report, for example, we might find nouns related in terms of a hierarchy, or in terms of part/whole relationships, or in terms of similarities or differences. In a story, on the other hand, relationships might be developed more through collocation and allusion. Text connectives will also differ according to the purpose of the text. An argument or discussion might employ connectives such as 'firstly', 'on the one hand', and 'in conclusion'. An explanation might include connectives which indicate causality and condition, such as 'so', 'therefore', 'if ... then'. A recount will typically use text connectives which help to sequence the events, such as 'then', 'afterwards', and 'eventually'. As readers, are the students able to exploit all these cohesive devices to follow the development of the text? And as writers, are they employing these devices in a way that makes their texts easier for the reader to follow?

Early Primary

Learning to ...

Most students should be able to structure a simple oral text appropriately (eg recounting in chronological order the events of the previous day; telling someone how to carry out a procedure in sequential steps). Students should be able to write a small range of familiar text types which are structured appropriately. When writing longer texts, they should demonstrate an awareness of the need to use paragraphs. Their written texts might have many of the features of spoken language (eg lacking the explicit and tight cohesion and text organisation typical of written language).

Learning about ...

Students should be able to discuss in broad, basic terms how a simple, familiar text has been organised. They should be able to recognise certain simple grammatical features typical of a particular text type. They can identify paragraph breaks. They should be able to recognise when the predictable organisation of familiar text types is disrupted (eg if the resolution were omitted from a story, or if a recount were sequenced incorrectly).

Mid Primary

Learning to ...

Students will be able to structure a wider range of oral and written texts appropriately according to the purpose of the text. They will be able to employ grammatical features and vocabulary which are appropriate to the text type. They will use paragraphs to organise the subject matter of their written texts. Their use of topic sentences, theme and text connectives might be somewhat rudimentary. Their written texts will display a greater control over cohesive devices (eg referring words and word associations), sounding less like spoken language.

Learning about

Students should be able to discuss the typical organisational structure of a basic range different text types, referring by name to the various stages of the texts. They should be able to identify some of the grammatical features which are characteristic of a particular text type. They should be able to trace the links in a text between various basic cohesive devices (eg pronouns referring back to a noun group). They should be able to identify the relationships between certain words in a text (eg words with a similar meaning, words with an opposite meaning, words which often occur together, words which form a 'set').

Later Primary

Learning to ...

Students should be using a wide range of text types (both oral and written) which are well structured to achieve their purpose. The grammatical patterns and vocabulary choices should contribute towards making the texts appropriate and effective. Written texts should be carefully crafted, with thought given to paragraphing, topic sentences, theme, and text connectives. In their reading, students should be able to exploit the various text organising features (text connectives, theme, cohesive devices) to make the developing meaning of the text more accessible. They should be able to appreciate the enriching power of such strategies as similes, metaphor and allusion, particularly in literary texts.

Learning about ...

Students should be able to reflect on and discuss the ways in which different text types are typically structured — as well as recognise that not all texts follow the typical pattern. They should be familiar with the characteristic grammatical features of various text types — and should be aware of how these predictable patterns can be changed and manipulated to produce a particular effect. They should be able to identify topic sentences in paragraphs. They should be familiar with a range of different text connectives and the role they play in structuring a text. They should be using terms such as 'synonym', 'antonym', 'simile' and 'metaphor' to refer to how words and ideas are related.

Revisiting the functions of language

8

In the Introduction, we looked at language from a functional perspective and saw that language does a number of different jobs. Halliday proposes three major functions of language:

- to enable us to interact with others (the 'interpersonal' function)

- to represent our experience of the world (the 'experiential' function)

- to create texts which are cohesive and coherent (the 'textual' function)

The sections one to seven provide understandings of the various language resources available in the English grammatical system. We can organise them in a different way, according to how they function. On the following pages, you will find a summary of

(i) those language resources we draw on when interacting with others. Our choices will be influenced by the tenor of the particular situation, eg what kind of role are we adopting (eg expert, adult, client, parent)? what kind of relationship are we trying to construct through language (eg intimate, impersonal, judgemental, antagonistic, submissive, tentative, authoritative)?

(ii) those language resources we draw on in representing our experience of the world. Our choices will be influenced by the field being developed (eg everyday, familiar understandings; abstract concepts; technical knowledge; in different areas of the curriculum; factual or literary; and so on).

(iii) those language resources we draw on in constructing texts which are coherent and cohesive. Our choices will be influenced by the channel of communication (or mode) being used (eg oral language accompanying action; prepared oral presentation; relaxed writing; reflective writing?)

(i) Language for interacting with others

	Form	Function	Example
Word and group level *Noun group* *Verb group* *Adverbials*	*Modality:* modal nouns & adjectives modal verbs modal adverbs negatives	to indicate degree of definiteness	possible, possibility, probable, definite could, might, must, should perhaps, maybe, never, always, possibly, absolutely no, not
	Other interpersonal resources: evaluative nouns, adjectives, verbs, and adverbs	to present a point of view, e.g. judgement of behaviour, appreciation of aesthetics and expression of emotions and different degrees of intensity.	recklessness, ill-mannered, simpered, stupidly, exquisite, very boring
	personal pronouns (1st & 2nd person)	to develop an 'I/you' relationship	I, we, you, me, my, our, your, mine, ours, yours
	terms of address ('vocatives')	to indicate status or intimacy	My Lord, Nurse Handley, you silly old fool, Bazzer
Clause level	*Mood* • declarative clause (auxiliary + finite)	to make a statement	He went to bed early that night.
	• interrogative clause (finite + auxiliary)	to ask a question	Are you going to bed?
	• imperative clause (minus subject and auxiliary)	to give a command	Go to bed!
	• 'skewed' clauses	to make indirect statements, questions and commands	Could you turn off the light?
Text level	overall patterning of interpersonal features turn/move	to create a particular tenor (eg intimate, impersonal, judgemental, negative)	*term of address* — 'What is it, darling?' *statement* — said Mrs Fox quickly. 'softener' — 'I've just had a bit of an idea,' *personal pronoun* — Mr Fox said carefully. *question* — 'What?' they cried. 'Oh Dad, what is it?' *command* — 'Come on!' said Mrs Fox. 'Tell us quickly'. *negative judgements* — 'It's no good,' he said. 'It won't work after all.'

(ii) Language for representing our experience of the world

	Form	Function	Example
Word and group level *Noun group*	nouns pronouns	referring to people, places, things, concepts ('participants')	Hannah, babies, home, Sydney, trees, happiness, time he, she, it, they, him, her, them
	adjectivals • articles, pointing words, possessives • different kinds of adjectives • adjectival phrases • adjectival clauses	describing people, places, things, concepts, eg 'which one?'; 'how many?'; 'whose?'; 'what qualities?'; 'what type?'; 'more information?'	that, those, many, his, their, Peter's, two, sad, wonderful, black, square, diesel, ...with the straw hat, ...who was caught in the rain *Noun group:* those two old hunting **dogs** with the droopy tails
Verb group	verbs + tense and number	indicating processes of acting/doing, thinking, feeling, wanting, saying, having, being, existing	runs, knew, hated, wished, commented, has, was, exists *Verb group:* have been thinking, was going to write, will be
Adverbials	adverbs adverbial phrases	giving information about the circumstances surrounding the above processes: how? when? where? why? by what means? with whom? in what role? like what?	quickly, now, very quietly, at dawn, in the garden, due to ill health, with a knife, with her mother, as a parent, like a songbird
Clause level	different combinations of nouns, verbs and adverbials	representing different aspects of experience (involving a process, the participant/s in that process, and any circumstance/s surrounding that process)	The boys raced up the corridor. She announced her retirement with some sadness. Kim had five frogs.
Combined clause level	clause combinations: • co-ordination (or compound) (+ co-ordinating conjunctions) • subordination (or complex) (+ subordinating conjunctions)	indicating the relationship between messages by: • combining messages of equal status (eg in terms of addition, contrast) • combining messages of unequal status (eg in terms of time, condition, purpose, reason, result, concession, place, manner)	and, but, or, nor, then, yet She has a full-time job **and** works at weekends too. before, if, so, although, where I would have gone **if** I had felt well enough.
	• projection	• reporting what people say or think	Jerry said that he didn't want to go. They thought they would be late.
Text level	the typical kinds of noun groups, verbs, and adverbials found in different text types	building up the subject matter (or 'field')	

(iii) Language for creating cohesive and coherent texts

	Form	Function	Example
Clause level	sentence focus/theme of clause/beginning of clause	to indicate the 'point of departure' of a message	**Marine creatures** *Theme* Fish are cold-blooded water-living animals. → *synonyms* They have <u>fins</u> on their body. → *part/whole* These help to guide them through the <u>water</u>. → *repetition* Some fish live in <u>fresh water</u>, → *antonyms* others live in the <u>sea</u>. Most fish lay eggs. → *collocation* Some, however, bear their <u>young</u> live. → *text connective*
	passive voice	to order information in a particular way	
Text level	topic sentences thematic development	to organise the flow of information in a text	
	cohesive devices	to establish links/relationships within a text	
	• referring words	• to link back to something already mentioned	
	• word associations	• to indicate links between content words in the text (eg similarities, opposites, word sets, hierarchies); to develop relationships within the subject matter	
	– synonyms – antonyms – repetition – class-subclass relations – part-whole relations – collocation		
	• text connectives	• to signal to the reader how the text is developing and guide the reader through the text	

References

Adams, C.V.A. (1958) *Nature is my Hobby*, Exeter, UK: A. Wheaton Publishers.

Bancroft, Bronwyn & Robinson, Roland (1996) *The Whalers*, Pymble: HarperCollins.

Cartwright, Pauline (1988) *What is it Like to be Old?* Petone, NZ: Highgate/Price Milburn.

Condon, Bill (1990) *That Smell is My Brother*, Marrickville: Harcourt Brace Jovanovich.

Davidson, Avelyn (1984) *Understanding Mathematics 5: How Many*, Auckland: Shorthand Publications.

Drew, David (1987) *Caterpillar Diary*, Melbourne: Thomas Nelson.

Factor, June (1985) *All Right, Vegemite!* Melbourne: Oxford University Press.

Gallico, Paul (1991) *Glorious Cats*, London: Aurum Press Lts.

Goode, John (1984) *Cattle and Beef*, Sydney: Hodder & Stoughton.

Grahame, Kenneth (1983; 1908) *The Wind in the Willows* (abridged by Barbara Sleigh), Kent, UK: Hodder & Stoughton.

Klein, Robin (1988) *Boss of the Pool*, Ringwood: Penguin.

Lawson, Henry (1985) *Humorous Stories of Henry Lawson*, Ryde: Angus & Robertson, Harper Collins.

Lear, Edward (1988; 1894) *Edward Lear's Nonsense Omnibus*, Leicester: Galley Press.

Milligan, Spike (1971) *Milligan's Ark*, Surrey: M&J Hobbs.

Milne, A.A. (1996; 1928) *The House at Pooh Corner*, Suffolk: Chancer Press.

Park, Ruth (1985) *Playing Beatie Bow*, Ringwood: Penguin.

Saxby, Maurice (ed) (1994) *My Country*, Melbourne: Macmillan.

Talese, G. in Eschholz, P. & Rosa, A. (eds) (1985) *Subject and Strategy*, New York: St Martins Press.

Wall, Dorothy (1985; 1939) *The Complete Adventures of Blinky Bill*, Ryde: Angus & Robertson.

Weston, Graham (1982) *Young Engineer in the Home*, East Sussex, UK: Wayland Publishers Ltd.

Wilson, Gina (1994) *Prowlpuss*, London: Walker Books.

(1996) *The Bunyip*, Board of Studies NSW and DET NSW.

Further reading

Allsop, J. (1989) *Making Sense of English Grammar*, London: Cassell.

Butt, D., Fahey, R., Spinks, S. and Yallop, C. (1995) *Using Functional Grammar: An Explorer's Guide*, Sydney:National Centre for English Language and Teaching Research.

COBUILD (1990) *English Grammar*, London: HarperCollins.

Collerson, J. (1994) *English Grammar: A Functional Approach*, Sydney: PETA.

Collerson, J. (1997) *Grammar in Teaching*, Sydney: PETA.

Cope, B. and Kalantzis, M. (eds) (1993) *The Powers of Literacy: A Genre Approach to Teaching Writing*, London: The Falmer Press.

Cusworth, R. (1994) *What is a functional model of language?* PEN 95, Sydney: PETA.

Derewianka, B. (1991) *Exploring How Texts Work*, Sydney: PETA.

Eggins, S. (1994) *An Introduction to Systemic Functional Linguistics*, London: Pinter.

Gerot, L. & Wignell, P. (1994) *Making Sense of Functional Grammar*, Sydney: AEE.

Halliday, M.A.K. (1994) *An Introduction to Functional Grammar* (2nd edition), London: Edward Arnold.

Halliday, M.A.K. (1985) *Spoken and Written Language*, Geelong: Deakin University Press.

Knapp, P. & Watkins, M. (1994) *Context – Text – Grammar*, Sydney: Text Productions.

Leech, G. & Svartvik, J. (1994) *A Communicative Grammar of English* (2nd edition) London: Longman.

Lock, G. (1996) *Functional English Grammar: An introduction for second language teachers*, Cambridge: Cambridge University Press.

Martin, J.R., Matthiessen, C., Painter, C. (1997) *Working with Functional Grammar*, London: Arnold.

McEvedy, M. (1996) *Learning Grammar in Context*, Melbourne: Thomas Nelson Australia.

Thompson, Geoff (1996) *Introducing Functional Grammar*, London: Edward Arnold.

Williams, G. (1993) 'Using systemic grammar in teaching young learners: an introduction', in L. Unsworth (ed.) *Literacy Learning and Teaching: Language as Social Practice in the Primary School*, Melbourne: Macmillan.